SOCIAL EXPERIENCE IN AFRICAN LITERATURE

Essays

Social Experience In African Literature

Essays

By

Oladele Taiwo

Fourth Dimension Publishing Co., Ltd.

First Published 1986 by
FOURTH DIMENSION PUBLISHING CO., LTD
16 Fifth Avenue, City Layout. PMB. 01164, Enugu, Nigeria.
Tel+234-42-459969. Fax+234-42-456904.
email: fdpbooks@aol.com, fdpbooks@yahoo.com
Web site: http://www.fdpbooks.com.

Reprinted 2002

© Oladele Taiwo 1978

ISBN 978-156-136-X

CONDITIONS OF SALE

All rights reserved. No part of this Publication may be reproduced, stored in a retrieval system, or transmitted in any form or by any means, electronic, mechanical, photocopying, recording, or otherwise without the prior permission of the Publisher.

Design and Typesetting by
Fourth Dimension Publishers, Enugu

CONTENTS

Page

Preface i

Acknowledgements iii

Chapter
1. Vital Issues in the Criticism of African Literature 1
2. The Essentials of Amos Tutuola's Narrative Art 15
3. The Nigerian Novel and the Problems of Communication .. 31
4. The Link between Tradition and Modern Experience in the Nigerian Novel 47
5. T. M. Aluko: The Novelist and His Imagination 69
6. Varieties of English in Nkem Nwankwo's Novels 95
7. The Use of Comedy in Nigerian Fiction 113
8. Drama in Education: An Analysis of Three Plays 125
9. The Women Novelists of West Africa 137
10. Language and Theme in Three African Novels 153

PREFACE

The ten essays collected in this volume were written at different times during a period of six years. They were published in learned journals in various parts of the world and each of them made an immediate impact on publication. Among them they discuss in detail several literary problems which arise from the new African Literature and examine critically the contributions of major writers like Amos Tutuola, Chinua Achebe, Wole Soyinka, Elechi Amadi, Gabriel Okara, T. M. Aluko, Meja Nwangi, Cyprian Ekwensi, Ola Rotimi, Ama Ata Aidoo and Alex La Guma. The works of other writers like Onuora Nzekwu, Adaora Ulasi, Obi Egbuna, Tafawa Balewa, Nkem Nwankwo, Flora Nwapa, and D. O. Olagoke are also considered. In bringing these articles together in one volume, the intention is to make them readily available to old and new readers.

The approach here is to examine critically vital issues in the criticism of African Literature and highlight those matters which will remain of considerable interest to critics for many years to come. These issues include the problems of communication in African Literature, the varieties of English in particular works, the intimate connection between language and meaning, the link between tradition and contemporary experience, the relevance of sociological material and the issue of the universality of a work of art. Some of these points are considered in detail in specific articles. Other articles are devoted to equally important matters as comedy in fiction, drama in education and the contribution of female novelists. One full-length article is devoted to Amos Tutuola and another to T. M. Aluko.

An attempt is made in this collection to put each writer in proper literary and historical perspective in African Literature, judged for the most part, by the writer's attitude to indigenous culture and the degree of success with which he has treated those aspects of African life he has chosen to dramatise. To start with, there are writers like Amos Tutuola and Tafawa Balewa, whose attitude to indigenous culture is one of near uncritical acceptance. Their language, for this reason, is either a transliteration of the mother tongue (L1) into English or one which exploits to the utmost, the resources of L1. Then, there are writers like Onuora Nzekwu, Adaora Ulasi, and Obi Egbuna whose main pre-occupation appears to be to propagate the customs and lore of their people. Their writings are at times overloaded with sociological material and embody obvious artistic faults. On the other hand, writers like Mejá Nwangi and Alex La Guma attach equal importance to content and language. They write about politically sensitive issues and racially disturbed parts of Africa. Their anxiety is adequately reflected in the conception and language of their works.

This volume has a unity of its own. This is provided by the identifiable characteristics of successful African writings which are stressed in nearly all the essays. These characteristics are, understandably, more obvious in the works of prominent writers like Chinua Achebe, Wole Soyinka, Ama Ata Aidoo and Ola Rotimi. They include an important theme, a consistent imaginative scheme, a language which recognises the potentials of L1 and skill in the use of language. Only works which embody all or many of these characteristics have the chance of giving artistic pleasure to readers and critics. These features provide necessary guidelines for beginning writers who may wish to dramatise in their works the social realities and dilemmas of contemporary African society.

I would like to thank the editors of the various journals who gave permission for the articles here to be reproduced. These articles have in a few cases been slightly amended. I also thank the publishers of this volume for their help and encouragement. I hope the book will satisfy the needs of students, teachers, critics, scholars, researchers and general readers working in the area of African Literature.

OLADELE TAIWO

January, 1982

ACKNOWLEDGEMENTS

These essays were first published as follows:

1. "Vital Issues in the Criticism of African Literature," in *African Literature: The State of Criticism*, Ime Ikiddeh, editor.
2. "The Essentials of Amos Tutuola's Narrative Art," *The Literary Half-Yearly* (Mysore, India) Vol. XVII, No. 1, January 1976, pp. 57—75.
3. "The Nigerian Novel and the Problems of Communication," in *Lagos Review of English Studies*, Vol. II, T. Vincent, editor.
4. "The Link between Tradition and Modern Experience in the Nigerian Novel," *Studies in Black Literature*, (Virginia, U.S.A.), Vol. 5, No. 3, 1974, pp. 11—16.
5. "T. M. Aluko: The Novelist and His Imagination," *Presence Africaine*, Paris, New Bilingual Series, No. 90, 1974, pp. 225—246.
6. "Varieties of English in Nkem Nwankwo's Novels," *Varieties and Functions of English in Nigeria*, edited by Ebo Ubahakwe (AUP and NESA, 1979), pp. 54—76.
7. "The Use of Comedy in Nigerian Fiction," *The Literary Half-Yearly* (Mysore, India), Vol. XV, No. 2, July 1974, pp. 107—120.
8. "Drama in Education: An Analysis of Three Plays," in *JNESA*, S. O. Unoh, editor.
9. "The Women Novelists of West Afria," *West African Studies in Modern Language Teaching and Research*, edited by Ayo Banjo, Conard Max, Benedict Branne, Henri Evans (The National Language Centre, Federal Ministry of Education, Lagos, 1981), pp. 199—211.
10. "Language and Theme in Three African Novels," *The Literary Half-Yearly* (Mysore, India) Vol. XXII, No. 1, January 1981, pp. 29—45.

The author wishes to thank the editors of these journals who have kindly given permission for the use of copyright material.

CHAPTER 1
VITAL ISSUES IN THE CRITICISM OF AFRICAN LITERATURE*

I.

The criticism of African Literature has gone on actively for about twenty years and has passed through several stages. The early stages were naturally characterized by uncertainties. The American and European critics, taken aback by the strange mode of the imagination displayed by the African, tried to solve all problems of criticism by finding parallels in their own Literatures. Furthermore, in an attempt to judge the new Literature by the motivation and orientation of the old, literary godfathers were appointed for African writers — Chinua Achebe drew on Hardy; J. P. Clark, on Hopkins; Okigbo, on Ezra Pound. This type of criticism proved so unhelpful that it was soon dropped.

The new writing at the early stages, for historical reasons, concerned itself mainly with culture conflict, the result of the attempt to impose European culture on the African. But since the middle sixties, the emphasis has shifted from the dramatization of culture contact to a detailed description and discussion of African social and economic problems. This has necessitated a new approach to criticism, which, in turn has raised a number of problems. The purpose of this article, is to highlight some of the vital issues which continue to engage the attention of the critic of the new African Literature.. The purpose is not to offer any permanent solutions — this is an area of work which hardly admits of solutions — but to throw some light on what must remain the pre-occupation of critics for many years to come.

II.

The question of who is qualified to criticise African Literature has been much discussed. Once African Literature is introduced into the main stream of World Literature, it should be possible for Africans and non-Africans alike to criticize it. Any critic capable

---

*First published in *African Literature: The State of Criticism*, edited by Ime Ikeddeh.

2 Social Experience in African Literature

of judging the works against the social and cultural background against which they are written should feel free to write about them. But how does the critic acquire this capability? The answer is simple and clear: the incisive knowledge required to criticize African Literature, can only come through patient learning and research on the part of the critic. Given the present orientation of the new Literature — its pre-occupation with Africa's past history and involvement with other continents, and the detailed analysis of the tensions and contradictions of present-day Africa — it must be allowed that the most beneficial insights into African Literature are likely to come from critics who have had the same experiences as those described by the authors. For, as Abiola Irele has said:

> Criticism cannot be pure scholarship and is not simply an intellectual exercise. I believe the best criticism implies an effective and intense participation in the creative act. The most worthy and enduring appreciation of the writer's work is that which partakes in the imaginative process in which the senses are alive to the verbal signposts which the writer has planted along the path to his profound intentions.[1]

It is important that the critic interprets correctly the "verbal signposts", which a particular author has utilised in his attempt to dramatize selected aspects of the life of his people. Otherwise, the work of criticism may fail in its main purpose of seeking answers to a number of searching questions: what are the particular values the writer is upholding or opposing? And what is his attitude to them? What particular emotional or intellectual effect does he hope to achieve? And does he succeed? If he does, by what method of communication? If he fails, from what problems of communication has failure resulted? And what effect does this have on the reader? For criticism to give a true reflection of the work of art, the critic must understand thoroughly not only the language of the author but also the socio-cultural circumstances surrounding the work. The critic, African or foreign, who is not willing to work hard quickly betrays his insufficient knowledge. When for example, Ola Rotimi says:

---

[1] "The Criticsm of Modern African Literature," *Perspectives on African Literature*, ed, Christopher Heywood (London, 1971), p. 14.

A son is a son: a husband is a husband. A woman cannot love both equally. Everything has its own place. Why, the tortoise is not tall but it is taller than the snail; the snail is taller than the frog; the frog is taller than the lizard; the lizard is taller than the fly; the fly is taller than the ant; the ant in turn is taller than the ground on which it walks. Everything has its own place, its own level, its standing.[2]

He is not only underlining the irony on which *The Gods Are Not to Blame* is constructed, but he is also stressing the hierarchical nature of the society he is writing about. The objects used serve here only as symbols. They are the "verbal signposts", with which the author makes his comparison and contrast. Even though it is possible for any perceptive critic to appreciate the contribution of this passage to the play as a whole, his work can become more valuable if he has some personal knowledge of each of the objects mentioned. Only then, can he fully realise what value has been attached to height. The taller objects are at the same time the more valuable ones, which leads us to appreciate how careful and accurate the playwright has been in his choice of words like tortoise, snail, frog, lizard and fly.

The work of criticism is undoubtedly advanced by a coincidence of feeling and experience between the writer and his critic. This seems particularly relevant to African Literature, dominated as it is by oral tradition. The influence of the writer's first language is usually not far from the surface. Vernacular words are often retained and occasionally they bear idiomatic meanings. Writers resort frequently to the resources of their first language and successfully dramatize the relevance of the past to the present, as Achebe does in this passage from the Egwugwu trial scene in *Things Fall Apart*:

> "Uzowulu's body, I salute you," he said,
> "Our father, my hand has touched the ground," replied Uzowulu, touching the earth.
> "Uzowulu's body, do you know me?"
> "How can I know you, father? You are beyond our knowledge," Uzowulu replied.

---

[2] *The Gods Are Not to Blame* (London, 1971), p. 38.

> "I am Evil Forest. I kill a man on the day that his life is sweetest to him."
> "That is true," replied Uzowulu.
> "Go to your in-laws with a pot of wine and beg your wife to return to you. It is not bravery when a man fights with a woman." He turned to Odukwe, and allowed a brief pause.
> "Odukwe's body, I greet you," he said.
> "My hand is on the ground," replied Odukwe.
> "Do you now me?"
> "No man can know you," replied Odukwe.
> "I am Evil Forest, I am Dry-meat-that-fills-the-mouth, I am Fire-that-burns-without-faggots. If your in-law brings wine to you, let your sister go with him. I salute you." He pulled his staff from the hard earth and thrust it back.
> "Umofia Kwenu!" he roared, and the crowd answered.[3]

It is the dignity of the scene which impresses the reader most. But this dignity may be missed by a foreign critic, who is not used to rituals of this kind. It is evoked by details such as the formality of address, the repetition of certain conventional statements and answers, the willing performance of ritualistic acts like touching the ground as a sign of total submission to the egwugwu and the orderliness of the whole procedure. Again, to show how rooted in Igbo tradition the scene is in content and language, the cognomens used are presented as direct translations from the Igbo original. The whole passage relies heavily on the linguistic characteristics of Igbo and Igbo speech rhythm in order that the various statements and responses may be "in character". These points are easily recognized and appreciated by an African critic willing to get at the facts. But the foreign critic, who merely attempts to relate to African Literature, the general principles derived from the criticism of European Literature, is likely to miss the significance of a scene like this and therefore, misinterpret the intentions of the author.

The foreign critic, who is unwilling to learn is exposed to many other errors of judgement. He stands the danger of becoming what Achebe has called a colonialist critic:

> I am going to use the word "colonialist" to describe a form of

---

[3] *Things Fall Apart* (London, 1969), pp. 84–85.

pseudo-literary criticism which is still very much alive today in African Literature and which derives from the same basic attitude and assumption as colonialism itself. This attitude and assumption was crystallised in Albert Schweitzer's immortal dictum: The African is indeed my brother, but my junior brother. The colonialist critic prompted by similar reasoning believes that the African writer is a somewhat unfinished European, who with patient guidance will grow up one day and write like every other European, but meanwhile must be humble, must learn all he can and give due credit to his teachers in the form of either direct praise or even better, such praise can become tricky and embarrassing self-contempt.[4]

What Achebe is complaining about here is the insidious attempt of some critics to judge African works by European standards, thus, denying these works of any individuality of their own. Colonialist critics conceive of African writings as an overseas extension of European Literature and therefore, fail to realise the need to adjust their sights. In actual fact, the criticism of modern African Literature can only be relevant and useful, when it takes into consideration the motivation and the cultural background against which it is written. Only critics, African or foreign, who respect the individuality, integrity and uniqueness of the new African Literature can hope to lead others to find useful and original insights in it.

III.

The problem of universality has remained a vital issue in literary criticism for a long time, but seems to have assumed prominence with the emergence of African writing. The erroneous impression has been created that the test of universality is more important for African writings than others. This, in itself, has raised other questions. What is the best, way of testing the effectiveness of a new literature? Why should beginning writers be concerned with universality? Can committed writers, with an urgent message, hope

---

[4] "Colonialist Criticism," paper presented at the 1974 Commonwealth Literature Conference at Makerere, Kampala, p. 1.

to achieve universality? Is it not attained only in a state of emotional stability? Is universality not, in fact, a stage of refinement reached only after many years of practice? The critic should see universality as part of the total framework within which Literature operates. It must not be conceived of as something which operates outside prose, poetry of drama to make the work acceptable. Universality is best judged by the extent to which a work of art extends our knowledge of the condition of man in society. Writers naturally write about the conditions they know well. Achebe, for example, is preoccupied largely with the traditional life of the Igbo as he came in contact with Western civilization. Onuora Nzekwu writes about Nigerian tribal society from the viewpoint of a fully-initiated member. Timothy Aluko scrutinizes different aspects of Yoruba culture. Tutuola assembles and embellishes Yoruba folk tales and shows through his writing the potentialities of African folklore and mythology as a vitalising force in Nigerian Literature. Other African writers show with varying degrees of success how proverbs, tales, myths, community festivals, traditional ceremonies, music and dancing can be exploited by the writer for his creative concern.

What is important is that the writer, starting from the local and particular, should reach the universal. The characters he portrays, the events he describes, the situations he generates in his work should reflect universal concern. It must be seen how the local events described have relevance for other parts of the world. This undoubtedly has been admirably achieved by many African writers. Amadi's works provide us with classic examples. His greatest achievement in *The Concubine*, for instance, lies in the fact that he uses the novel to criticize life at a symbolic level. His realistic description of life at Omokachi village serves only as a basis for making a statement of more than local significance. The novel is concerned with the circumstances of a marriage which ends in disaster for reasons which are deeply human and universally valid. This disaster is made to appear as unavoidable as it is startling. The reader is persuaded in the end that tragedy is inevitable because of the formidable forces against which Ekwueme and Ihuoma have had to contend; that, given similar forces, no marriage could be expected to survive anywhere, any time.

The same type of universal concern is shown in *The Great Ponds* where, mainly through the detailed presentation of disappointed hopes, Amadi builds up the overall impression of the futility of war. Chiolu and Aliakoro devote all their resources to fighting a war over the Great Ponds, and in the process, bring untold hardship to their people. To the villagers, these events must have been of world significance, since their mental horizon is limited only to the village. The reader, however, is inclined to attach only local significance to them initially, before the message of the novel begins to dawn on him. The dreadful disease of wonjo has afflicted a number of villages, causing widespread distress, and the villagers sincerely hope the end of their suffering is in sight when we are told: "But it was the beginning. Wonjo, as the villagers called the Great Influenza of 1918, was to claim a grand total of some twenty million lives all over the world."[5] By the allusion and the date quoted, a tacit comparison between the events of *The Great Ponds* and those of the Great War is implied, and the greater significance of the work becomes unmistakable. The war of the Great Ponds then emerges as part of a world-wide pattern. The success of the novel, is owed mainly to this use of the details of village life to make a symbolic statement of such tragic significance.

Universality derives, partly, from the imaginative grasp and artistic intelligence displayed by a writer. Where several events of a work of art fully exploit a particular background and are integral to the life the writer is trying to create in his work, these events can be said to be truly local. If they are such that can be applied to similar situations in other parts of the world, they then become truly universal. For,

> Much more fundamental than the mere reproduction of syntax is the conveying in its totality of an experience in a way that reflects its environment without precluding it from general applicability. In looking at the African author's work, we may be able to see its universality. Fortunately, the two things often go together. A work which succeeds in realising its environment to the full, often achieves this universality. The happy paradox is that, to be truly universal, one must be truly local.[6]

A work of art cannot be said to lack universality, merely, because it is based on an African setting or to operate automatically within

---

[5] *The Great Ponds* (London, 1970), p. 217.
[6] Eldred Jones "The Decolonisation of African Literature" *The Writer in Modern Africa*, ed. Per Wastberg (Uppsala, 1968), p. 73.

a universal framework only because the setting is European or American. Much more important than the setting is the creative intelligence shown by the writer.

IV.

Other vital issues in the criticism of African Literature concern the relevance of sociological material, the distance in time and place which the author should keep between him and his material, the problem of language in African Literature and how rigorous the standard of criticism applied to African writings should be. Some of these are more important than others. A few of them are easily disposed of.

Given the necessary inspiration and creative energy, a writer can write successfully about his times and his contemporary world. Dipoko, Peters, Achebe, Ngugi wa Thiong'o are a few of the writers who have done this successfully. The danger, of course, is there, and only the best writers are able to avoid it. Unless the writer succeeds in achieving some degree of detachment from the events he describes, he may intrude into them in a manner capable of destroying the basis of art. Each writer devises his own methods of achieving such detachment. For example, the technical complexity of *A Man of the People*, arises from Achebe's use of Odili as heronarrator. The novelist uses Odili to satirize political institutions and the people, but he often satirizes Odili himself. Achebe looks at society for the most part through Odili's eyes but often stands apart from Odili in order to observe him critically. In this way the reader's response to Odili is directed with sustained subtlety. We find ourselves attracted to him or repelled by him according to how close or far he is at any given moment to his proclaimed moral position. Achebe's ability to detach himself purposefully from the situation he describes, when necessary, represents a great achievement in the novel. For according to Arthur Gakwandi:

> When an African writer attempts to depict the crises of his contemporary world he has to struggle to free himself from the anxieties, the fears and the hysterias of his time. If he does not free himself... he may find himself part of the mass hysteria, pronouncing popular and second rate judgements and creating generalised figures instead of living human characters

... when this happens the reader is left no wiser than he was, apart from learning that there is an artist who has gone neurotic.[7]

Distance in time and place is not absolutely necessary for artistic success. What is important is that the writer, when trying to explain the dilemmas of his contemporary world, should stand aside from popular judgements, free himself from the hysterical reactions of his society and avoid empty sloganizing.

V.

Considering the circumstances of the new writing, the use of sociological material cannot altogether be avoided. What the critic should concern himself with, is the use made of sociological material in a piece of work. When facts are presented in a literal fashion, they tend to obscure the writer's intention and interfere with his artistic purpose. If one considers *Wind versus Polygamy*, for example, as an artistic failure, it is because of the author's indulgence in overt documentary excessiveness to the detriment of a fully-realized relevant environment. Instead of integrating sociological passages into the living situation of the novel, the novelist gives them an existence independent of art. He shows an inclination to explain rather than to create life in the novel. The same fault is found in, *Wand of Noble Wood*, which contains many examples of tiresomely explicit sociological material:

> Among us, kola-nut is a highly valued and indispensable product. It commands our respect in a way no other produce has done. Though it is one of the commonest vegetable products seen in Nigeria, it represents, in our society, a vital social and religious element. Kola-nut is a symbol of friendship, the proper offering at meetings and religious occasions. Its presentation to a guest surpasses any other sign of hospitality which any host among us can show, even though in some places it costs only a penny.[8]

---

[7] "Heroes and Villains of African Fiction," paper presented at the 1974 Commonwealth Literature Conference at Makerere, Kampala, p. 2.
[8] *Wand of Noble Wood* (London, 1971), p. 67.

This novel has been described by a reviewer as "almost a manual of popular anthropology"[9] because it has too many of such passages.
There are many writers, who use sociological material in a sound artistic way in their writing. Instead of showing an impulse to educate, Amadi, for example, dramatises a point in such a context that its importance is directly conveyed. This is the way in which Achebe in *Arrow of God*, establishes the importance of the New Yam Festival in the religious life of Umuaro. In the same manner, Amadi impresses upon the reader the importance of kola in an appropriate setting. The occasion is one which combines tradition and history, when Chiolu and Aliakoro meet after one of their usual encounters at the Great Ponds to talk about the ransom for prisoners of War. The image of past grandeur is evoked, as is appropriate on historic occasions, by the use of praise-names. It is into this important setting that Amadi introduces the importance of the Kola:

> Diali broke the kola, took one piece and offered the rest to Okehi. Again the kola did the rounds. The wooden bowl was almost empty by the time it got back to Diali. The Chief took one piece, broke it into smaller fragments and scattered them on the ground, thereby offering them to Amadioha, the god of thunder and of the skies, Ali, the earth god, Ojukwu, the Fair and Ogbunabali, the god who kills by night.[10]

Not only are the principal actors in the drama of *The Great Ponds*, willing to partake of the piece of the kola from the same bowl, even the gods are offered their fair share. Kola is thus, employed in the process of reconciling two warring villages on an occasion attended by god and man. Such a situation brings out more clearly the "vital social and religious element" of the kola than Nzekwu's documentary harangues. One is made to see just how and why it is important without explicit instruction.

VI.

The problem connected with the use of language in African Literature is so central that no discussion of it can be considered exhaustive or final. Each critic can only hope to make a little

---

[9] Review in *West Africa*, No. 2312, 23 September, 1961, p. 1053.
[10] *The Great Ponds* (London, 1970), p. 17.

contribution. In a second language Literature, the use of Language is affected by several factors — the artist's linguistic competence, the kind of material he is handling, what he intends to make of this material and the type of audience he has in mind. Although many of the writers of modern African Literature use English, they do so, conscious of the fact that they wish to convey typical African experiences. In order to make the language serve the purpose for which it was not originally designed, many new things have been done with it. We have a wide-spread range from the near illiterate English of Tutuola, the unorthodox pidgin English of Adaora Ulasi, to the language which expresses adequately the writer's sensibility in Achebe, Ngugi and Lenrie Peters, among others, and the experimental language of Okara. Most of the intentional deviations from standard English in Okara's works have resulted from the pursuit of the author's artistic purpose, or as a direct influence of his first language (L1). Where the influence of the mother tongue dominates the writer's language, as we see in Tutuola, the result is usually a kind of writing which concentrates more on ancestral values and implies, on the whole, little criticism of society, past and present. For this reason, the link with modern life is not always recognizable.

A writer, on the other hand, may be so anxious to avoid the influence of his first language that he writes the kind of English which defeats his artistic purpose. This seems to have been the case with Obi Egbuna in, *Wind versus Polygamy*. He has contributed nothing to the experimentation with English by African writers. His use of stilted language in the narrative and descriptive sections of the work, casts serious doubt on his creative intelligence. This is how the novel starts:

> A full moon and a blaze-red sun were just changing shifts over a quiet little village in the heart of New Africa. A tin-roofed cottage sat on top of a nameless hill as silently as the hibiscus flowers blossoming before it. The frontage of this peaceful house was where it all began. The twilight was golden. With the chirping of crickets for company and the domy blueness of the tropical sky before her eyes, Elina, an African girl of tantalizing beauty, sat like a tigress on a kitchen stool peeling yams in the moonlight.[11]

---

[11] *Wind versus Polygamy* (London, 1964), p. 7.

Apart from verbal infelicities – moon and sun "changing shifts", a cottage and hibiscus flowers "sat" on top of a hill – visualization is extremely poor, as is evident in the last sentence. Elina has for company "the chirping of crickets"; she "sat like a tigress" – "on a kitchen stool" – and only for the purpose of "peeling yams in the moonlight". If Egbuna had learnt the art of communicating local Nigerian concepts economically through a transliteration from L1, as Achebe does when describing a situation like this, a more acceptable picture might have been drawn. But his prose style, unlike that of most others Nigerian writers, owes little to L1. He appears on the whole more interested in dazzling the reader with exotic vocabulary than capturing the tone and relevant levels of speech of Igbo villagers.

The same kind of charge could be levelled against Miss Ulasi for her use of an unorthodox form of Pidgin English in *Many Thing You No Understand*. The quality of the Pidgin is often so poor that it constantly distracts the attention of the reader whose ears are attuned to good Pidgin:—

> "What you say you want?" the new Chief Obieze asked the messenger from MacIntosh.
> "Mr. A.D.O. he said he want you to see him face to face tomorrow when the hand for clock say ten o'clock."
> "What the A.D.O. say him want?"
> "Me no know, Chief Obieze."
> "You think it be for anything bad?"
> "I no fit know. I be only messenger."
> "As you know, I still stay for mourning for my father. Many people still come to comfort me. I no like for them to come and me no be here for them to see and comfort."[12]

Practically every sentence here is wrong Pidgin. The first word "what" should be "wetin". "What" is not part of the vocabulary of Pidgin. The clumsiness of the second paragraph of the passage, resulting mainly from the use of both, "Mr. A.D.O." and the pronoun "he" side by side and the inclusion of unnecessary details like "face to face", "when the hand for clock say ten o'clock" is an indication of the author's limited knowledge of Pidgin, not

---

[12] *Many Thing You No Understand* (London, 1970), p. 92.

a fault inherent in the medium itself. What we have here is neither Standard English nor acceptable Pidgin. "Me no know", for example, is nearer Standard English than Pidgin. In standard Pidgin this would be, "I no sabi" and "I still stay for mourning for my father" should be "I still de mourn me fader". The whole passage lacks the fluency which a dialogue in Pidgin is capable of producing mainly because of the author's difficulty in communicating effectively in her chosen medium.

It is important to stress that, after the use of Pidgin in common speech and as a medium of creativity for several years, it has come to acquire its own special vocabulary and syntax, which are not often identical with those of Standard English. It is only when the unique features of Pidgin are recognized that it can serve as a useful medium of creativity. By using an unorthodox form of Pidgin, and often in the wrong situations, Miss Ulasi fails to communicate as effectively as she might have done, using a medium with which she is more familiar.

Criticism, to be useful, must bring out the debilitating effect on the author's contribution of such insensitive use of language, as one finds in Egbuna and Adaora Ulasi. It destroys the basis of true characterization and leads the critic to wonder whether when writing their books, these novelists had any clear idea of the social relationships between various characters. The critic, on the other hand, must be willing to recognize in Okara's use of words and symbols a successful experimentation with language. As in most of his poems, the significance of the various parts of *The Voice*, from which a clear statement finally emerges, dawns on the reader gradually because of the time it takes to decode the writer's symbols. As Charlotte Bronte points out:

> When authors write best, or, at least, when they write most fluently, an influence wakens in them which becomes their master which will have its own way — putting out of view all behests but its own...[13]

The motivating force, in Okara's case, is undoubtedly his desire to devise an English prose style, suitable for his immediate purpose.

---

[13] Letter to G. H. Lewes, 18 January, 1848 quoted in David Lodge, *The Language of Fiction* (London, 1966), p. 83.

VII.

Africa is experiencing a cultural rebirth which is reflected in the feverish literary activities of her writers. The fact, that this reawakening has had to be presented mostly in non-African Languages, poses very many basic problems for the critic, whose business it is to present these works to the reading public. The critic is called upon to consider all kinds of subjects and to give his criticism, like the writings he is considering, an African quality, an African character. He can only achieve this if, in his judgement, he gives due weight to the social and cultural motivation of the writers and the circumstances in history which helped to make the African environment what it is today. A blind application of what is usually vaguely referred to as universal standard of criticism may obscure the African dimension of a work of art. Unless criticism is related to a specific cultural framework, it becomes limited in scope and therefore, of little relevance. Again, as African Literature moves farther away from the ancestral shrine, the village green and mission school, and comes to grips with the age of Science and Technology, the problem of language is likely to become more acute, making the work of criticism even more complex.[14] In order to be able to do his work successfully, the African critic of the future will require, as part of the general preparation for his self-assigned role, not only an incisive knowledge of the customs, lore and way of life of the people he is writing about, but also the changes which have been brought upon their environment and circumstances of life by Science and Technology.

---

[14] See, for example, "The Task Ahead" Chapter 11, Oladele Taiwo, *An Introduction to West African Literature* (London, 1967).

CHAPTER 2
THE ESSENTIALS OF AMOS TUTUOLA'S NARRATIVE ART*

I.

Amos Tutuola is one of the most controversial of Nigeria's novelists. When his *The Palm-Wine Drinkard* was published in 1952 it was an instant success abroad, but was accorded very little recognition at home.[1] The foreign critics attached a great deal of importance to Tutuola's language and claimed that this had an unusual effect on the content of the book. But fellow-Nigerians initially denied him any claim to originality and objected to his Language.[2] According to Ulli Beier:

> Nigerian readers complained... that Tutuola wrote "wrong" English, that his books were a mere "rehash" of grandmother tales they had all heard before. They alleged that Europeans were merely attracted by the quaint exotic qualities of the book and that they did not judge the work on literary merits.[3]

---

*First published in *The Literary Half-Yearly* (Mysore, India) XVII, January 1, 1976, pp. 57–75.

[1] Tutuola now has six novels to his credit, all published by Faber and Faber, London. For convenience the shortened forms of the titles of four of the novels (given in brackets) are the ones used in this study:
    The Palm-Wine Drinkard, 1952.
    My Life in the Bush of Ghosts, 1954. (Bush of Ghosts)
    Simbi and the Satyr of the Dark Jungle, 1955. (Simbi)
    The Brave African Huntress, 1958.
    Feather Woman of the Jungle, 1962. (Feather Woman)
    Ajaiyi and His Inherited Poverty, 1967. (Ajaiyi)

[2] The two sides of the argument are well summed up by some previous writers. See, for example, Gerald Moore, "Amos Tutuola: A Modern Visionary," *Seven African Writers* (London, 1962), p. 39–57; Bernth Lindfors, "Amos Tutuola and D. O. Fagunwa," *The Journal of Commonwealth Literature* No. 9 (1970), p. 57–65; Omolara Leslie, "*The Palm-Wine Drinkard*. Reassessment of Amos Tutuola," *The Journal of Commonwealth Literature*, No. 9 (1970), p. 48–56. For the differences in initial reaction to Tutuola at home and abroad, compare, for example, Dylan Thomas's review of *The Palm-Wine Drinkard* in *Observer*, July 6, 1952, No. 8405 with references to Tututola in J. P. Clark, "Our Literary Critics," *Nigeria Magazine*, 74 (1962).

[3] Ulli Beier, "Nigerian Literature," *Nigeria Magazine*, Special Independence Issue (1960), p. 213.

In recent years, however, Nigerians have taken more kindly to Tutuola. The latest criticisms of his works have been far more favourable.[4] In this article an attempt will be made to assess the importance of Tutuola to the Nigerian Novel and determine the factors which have led to recent objective appraisals of his works. A good deal of attention will be paid to his narrative techniques, his powers of description, the intense oral quality of his prose and his imaginative inventiveness.

II.

In order to appreciate fully Tutuola's contribution to the Nigerian Novel, he must be seen as a writer standing between the old and the new, a writer active during a period of transition from a purely oral tradition of village story-telling to Western-introduced literary tradition. His greatest achievement is that, he represents a successful integration of both traditions. Both influences feature prominently in his works. The process of integration in each case seems to have been as follows: Tutuola takes a story in its well-known form, amends it to suit his artistic purpose, usually by introducing new characters and episodes and occasionally by introducing elements of modern life; this story in its new form is then worked into the framework of another much longer story which itself may have resulted from a combination of many stories reshaped by Tutuola's imagination. Stories are introduced into larger frameworks to serve various artistic purposes, and the whole process is carried out in such a highly imaginative way that the stories dovetail easily one into another. To cite an example, *Ajaiyi* is the story of Ajaiyi and his sister, Aina, who set out on a perilous journey to try to find out a cure for their inherited poverty. Into this framework are woven Tutuola's versions of other stories, one of which is the story of Ade's ingratitude to Ajaiyi. This story is introduced at the appropriate point to show the differences in character and moral orientation between Ajaiyi and Ade and is made to fit properly into the larger framework. That is why when one reads *Ajaiyi*,

---

[4]See, for example, A. Adetugbo, "Form and Style," *Introduction to Nigerian Literature*, ed. Bruce King (London, 1971), p. 176; Abiola Irele, "The Criticism of Modern African Literature," *Perspectives on African Literature*, ed. Christopher Heywood (London, 1971), p. 17.

one does not have a feeling of going through an anthology of stories but of a composite story into which other narratives have been wholly integrated. This is an essential of Tutuolan art which is missed by all those who claim that the structures of his works are too loose for them to be called novels. The traditional narrative form is usually self-contained. It is sufficient in itself for structure, style and purpose. What Tutuola does is to introduce artistically and successfully a number of these episodes into his writing. Some of the novels contain more episodes than others and these episodes hold together better in some novels than in others. But even one of the most episodic of the novels, *The Palm-Wine Drinkard*, has been shown to achieve narrative and intensive continuity through density "in much the same way... in which the discreet beats of drumming occur with such dense frequency as to create a temporal 'solid', or continuity."[5]

Another essential of the Tutuolan art is the use he makes of all the techniques available to the oral story-teller to make his stories interesting. Tutuola, as it were, does in writing what the story-teller does verbally before his audience. He is primarily "a story-teller in the best Yoruba tradition, pushing the bounds of credibility higher and higher and sustaining it by sheer adroitness, by a juxta-position of analogous experience from the familiar."[6] He gives us the true setting of traditional story-telling sessions in *Feather Woman* where he provides ten "night entertainments". In these "entertainments", story-telling is accompanied with drinking, dancing and drumming, as we have in this setting for the eighth night.

"And it was hardly nine o'clock of the eighth night, as the moon was just appeared, when the whole people of my village had gathered in front of my house. When all of them sat quietly then everyone was served with one keg of the palm-wine and the biggest keg was in front of me. After they had drunken some of their wine and then sung and danced for a while, and when I put the fire in my pipe and then sat up in my usual old armchair. Then, when the people sat back quietly and were ready to hear my story. I began to tell them the story of my sixth journey."[7]

---

[5] Robert P. Armstrong, "The Narrative and Intensive Continuity: The Palm-Wine Drinkard," *Researches in African Literatures*, Vol. 1, No. 1 (1970), p. 30.
[6] Wole Soyinka, "From a Common Back Cloth: A Reassessment of the African Literary Image". *AMSAC News-letter*, Vol. 6, No. 6 (1964), p. 5.
[7] *Feather Woman*, p. 104.

Just as the oral story-teller seeks to involve his audience in his narration by occasionally putting questions to them and inviting their participation, so also Tutuola uses various devices to involve his readers in his stories. In some cases, he puts direct fact questions to them as he does, for example, in connection with the woman who brings the Drinkard and his wife to the Red Town — "She was not a human-being and she was not a spirit but what was she?"[8] — or with reference to the problem posed by the "Lost or Gain Valley" — "So I am still eager to find out the right way of how to cross this 'Lost or Gain Valley' without any loss except gain. Do you know?"[9] Sometimes the question is rhetorical like the one used to justify Rali's reaction to the abduction of Simbi by an eagle — "If it were you or I, how in deep grief you or I would be?"[10] There is also Tutuola's use of dilemma tales to increase the reader's involvement with his novels. There are two very interesting ones in, *The Palm-Wine Drinkard*. In the "mixed town", the Drinkard is called upon to judge two cases, but he finds himself unequal to the task. Tutuola, therefore, decides to let his readers try their hand at judging these cases. "So I shall be very grateful," he says, "if anyone who reads this story-book can judge one or both cases and send the judgement to me as early as possible, because the whole people in the 'mixed town' want me very urgently to come and judge the two cases."[11] However, there are a few examples of happily-resolved dilemmas in the novels. An example is the one in *Ajaiyi*, which nearly results in the loss of Babi's daughter but for the generosity shown at the last minute by Aina.

Another device borrowed from traditional verbal art is the adoption of the point of view of a first-person narrator. With the exception of *Simbi*, all the novels of Tutuola are written in the first-person and this has made it possible, as it were, for him to "talk" direct to the reader. He uses this device to make up for the difference between the oral and written versions of the same story, usually resulting from what cannot naturally be committed to writing — voice, gestures and facial expression — to mention a few. This has been largely responsible for the intense oral quality of his writing. The combined effect of these two devices — first-person narration

---

[8] *The Palm-Wine Drinkard*, p. 83.
[9] *Bush of Ghosts*, p. 133.
[10] *Simbi*, p. 82.
[11] *The Palm-Wine Drinkard*, p. 115.

and his warm speaking voice of which a few examples will be cited presently — has been to increase the reader's interest in his novels and make the novels themselves more valuable as literature:

> First-person narration by the protagonist gives us the greatest possible sense of involvement in the story. Empathy is fully possible, so that we have the illusion of undergoing all the protagonist's adventures and sharing with him the revelations brought by his experience. His moral growth becomes, ideally, ours. This effect can be achieved with other points of view, but it is never so convincing as in first-person narration by the protagonist.[12]

The intense oral quality of Tutuola's writing is evident on practically every page of his novels. The peculiar rhythms of his English are the rhythms of Yoruba speech. However, the speaking voice is warmer in certain parts of his works than in others, and occasionally becomes captivating. At the beginning of *The Palm-Wine Drinkard*, one has the impression of a speaker speaking directly to another in front of him:

> I was a palm-wine drinkard since I was a boy of ten years of age. I had no other work more than to drink palm-wine in my life. In those days, we did not know other money, except COWRIES, so that everything was very cheap, and my father was the richest man in our town.
> My father got eight children and I was the eldest among them, all of the rest were hard workers, but I myself was an expert palm-wine drinkard. I was drinking palm-wine from morning till night and from night till morning. By that time I could not drink ordinary water at all except palm-wine.
> But when my father noticed that I could not do any work more than to drink, he engaged an expert palm-wine tapster for me; he had no other work more than to tap palm-wine everyday.[13]

Feather Woman provides very many examples of this type of

---

[12] Lynn Altenbernd and Leslie Lewis, *A Handbook for the Study of Fiction* (London, 1969), pp. 63–64.
[13] *The Palm-Wine Drinkard*, p. 7.

oral performance mainly because it is a collection of stories told to a group of enthusiastic listeners. This is how the entertainment of the third night begins:

> It was hardly nine o'clock of the third night, when the people of my village came to my house to enjoy the entertainment of my second adventure. All sat as usual and everyone was served with one keg of palm-wine. But this third night, they brought with them some drums, horns and many other of the native musical instruments, because we were badly disappointed about the musical instruments the first night. Then I sat on my usual old armchair in front of them. As the moon was shining and the cool breeze of that dry season was blowing very quietly. Then after everyone had drunken of his or her palm-wine and I put fire in my smoking pipe. I first addressed the people: "You see, my people, my motto this night is that this world is not equal. So all my adventures were not the same. One who has head, has no money to buy hat and one who has money to buy hat, has no head on which to put it."[14]

Tutuola uses the folktales in his novels in a progressive evolutionary manner.[15] To make them fully functional, he occasionally includes in them features of Western civilization. In doing this, he is acting within his right as a story-teller to amend the content of his tales to suit his purpose. He is at the same time establishing a connection between the past and present experiences of his people by creating a link in this way between tradition and modern life. What makes this point important in Tutuola, is the way he fully integrates Western elements into the texture of his works and makes successful artistic use of them. They have not only helped to broaden the base of his narrative and give the content of his novels a wider application, but have occasionally been utilized in plot management. At times they only help to make a point clearer as in the following cases in *The Palm-Wine Drinkard*: the half-

---

[14] *Feather, Woman*, p. 36.
[15] For a discussion of the evolutionary and devolutionary uses of folktales, see Alan Dundes, "The Devolutionary Premise in Folklore Theory," *Journal of the Folklore Institute*, Vol. 6, No. 1 (1969), pp. 5–19.

bodied baby speaks "with a lower voice like a telephone",[16] the Drinkard becomes "a big bird like an aeroplane"[17] and flies away with his wife to avoid highwaymen, the young lady who approaches the Drinkard and his wife after they have left the Faithful-Mother has on "high-heel shoes which resembled aluminium in colour"[18] In *Bush of Ghosts*, the "homeless-ghosts" listen to the cry of the hero-wandered "as a radio"[19] and in *Feather Woman*, the hero-narrator builds "a very beautiful storey which had many flats".[20] Often these comparisons result in felicitous expressions which provide some of the most delightful passages in the whole of the Tutuola canon, as we find in these two examples. In the first, the author makes use of the knowledge gained from his participation in the last world war:

> I could not blame the lady for following the Skull as a complete gentleman to his house at all. Because if I were a lady, no doubt I would follow him to wherever he would go, and still as I was a man I would jealous him more than that, because if this gentleman went to the battlefield, surely, enemy would not kill him or capture him and if bombers saw him in a town which was to be bombed, they would not throw bombs on his presence, and if they did throw it, the bomb itself would not explode until this gentleman would leave that town, because of his beauty.[21]

The second is an imaginative description of the Red Fish, which draws on the author's acquaintance with Western industrial civilization:

> At the same time that the red fish appeared out, its head was just like a tortoise's head, but it was as big as elephant's head and it had over 30 horns and large eyes which surrounded the head. All these horns were spread out as an umbrella. It could not walk but was only gliding on the ground like a

---

[16] P. 35.
[17] P. 40.
[18] P. 73.
[19] P. 50.
[20] P. 96.
[21] *The Palm Wine Drinkard*, p. 25.

snake and its body was just like a bat's body and covered with long red hair like strings. It could only fly to a short distance, and if it shouted a person who was four miles away would hear. All the eyes which surrounded its head were closing and opening at the same time as if a man was pressing a switch on and off.[22]

However, it is in their use for plot management that these Western elements have been of the greatest service to Tutuola. It is not known to what extent he was conscious of this, but it is a fact that by his use of Western ideas and institutions, he has been able to avoid in *Bush of Ghosts*, some of the errors of the structure of *The Palm-Wine Drinkard*. In *The Palm-Wine Drinkard*, except for brief period of rest with the Faithful-Mother, the Drinkard and his wife go from one dreadful experience to another. The hero-wanderer in *Bush of Ghosts*, after wandering in the Bush for twenty years, runs into a dead cousin of his in the tenth Town of Ghosts. Considering the length of time the boy has spent in the Bush and the harrowing experiences he has gone through, he badly needs some respite at the time he gets to the tenth Town of Ghosts. It seems reasonable to suppose one of the reasons he enjoys his stay with his cousin, and is able to remain with him for so long, is that his time is gainfully employed in the school and "as the chief judge of the highest court which is 'Assize court' ".[23] Far more important, is the way Tutuola brings this particular novel to an end by using a device which, although not Western, shows to what extent he is willing to incorporate Western-derived ideas into his stories: through the use of an "Invisible Magnetic Missive", the boy's mind is directed ho.neward and he is magically brought back home by looking at the palm of the Television-handed Ghostess. But for this device, it might have been necessary to get the hero-wanderer to go through some other adventures on his way home. Such unnecessary prolongation of the boy's monotonous experiences of horror, would have further weakened an already weak structure and virtually destroyed any impact the present book has. We would then have experienced, as is the case at the end of *The Palm-Wine Drinkard*, "a repetitive pattern of marvels... where the anecdotic functions are duplicated with the effect, sometimes, of crescendo and even

---
[22] *Ibid.*, pp. 79–80.
[23] *Bush of Ghosts*, p. 152.

boredom."[24]

The third essential of the Tutuolan art is the use of the guest form. This form is adapted to suit the particular requirements of each novel. In each of these novels, the hero is highly motivated by the object of his search and the conviction of the enormous advantages which will be derived from a mission successfully accomplished. This is what gives meaning and purpose to his journey and for this, he is usually willing to take risks and forego every kind of convenience. Hence, for example, the Drinkard sets out to find his dead tapster in the town of the dead. The pursuit of this objective takes the hero from the world of living beings to the world of the dead and results in a journey fraught with every kind of danger. Adebisi in *The Brave African Huntress*, sets out in order to rescue her four brothers from the jungle of the pigmies; the hero-narrator in *Feather Woman*, to seek wealth and Ajaiyi and Aina in *Ajaiyi*, to look for a cure for their inherited poverty. Each of these, is no doubt an important mission worthy of the hero's devotion. Simbi's mission is of a different kind; even so, it results in a journey just as hazardous as any other. She of her own volition, decides to go abroad in order to "experience the difficulties of the 'Poverty' and of the 'Punishment' ".[25] On the other hand, the hero-wanderer in *Bush of Ghosts*, gets into the Bush without wishing to and finds himself undertaking a long tedious journey in order to avoid the jealousies of his father's wives.

As soon Tutuola's heroes start their journeys, for whatever reasons, they begin to be faced with difficult tasks, many of which can only be accomplished by supernatural means. Usually, they are magically equipped to transform themselves into any object of their choice or otherwise, make themselves invisible to avoid being killed by the enemy. It is only the reader's knowledge that the heroes have these powers that assures him they will survive. Occasionally, the hero is given a little respite, a period of comfort and easy life during which he appears to have forgotten the object of his search. The Drinkard spends such a period with the Faithful-Mother; the wanderer in the Bush of Ghosts, with the Super Lady; Adebisi, in the Bachelors' Town and Simbi, with the old woman

---

[24] S. O. Anozie, "Structure and Utopia in Tutuola's *'Palm-Wine Drinkard'*" *The Conch*, No. 2, (1970), p. 86.
[25] *Simbi*, p. 9.

who gives her temporary shelter, But the hero soon pulls himself together again and continues with the object of his search in a single-minded manner, until he finally arrives at his goal a wiser man than he set out. In this way, Tutuola uses effectively, a rather simplified version of the quest form — a hero at one end and the object of his search at the other. In between are interposed difficult tasks, which make the objective of the hero almost impossible to accomplish. The only reason the hero perseveres, is the high motivation provided by the achievement of his goal; usually, the only way he can survive is by the use of his magical power. The advantage of the quest form is that it lends itself easily to episodic treatment. The hero is made to go from one adventure to another and the author is free to introduce any number of these. There can be no doubt that Tutuola makes the fullest use of this advantage in his novels.

III.

These three essentials are the advantages which Tutuola has derived from the integration of features of traditional verbal art into his novels. But also, in his attempt to impose literary organization on an essentially oral material, he has adopted certain techniques which will do any writer, however sophisticated, great credit. One such technique is his ability to create a tense atmosphere, and this is widely applied to great advantage in his novels. Take, for example, the tension created during the titanic struggles between the Drinkard and the Red Fish in *The Palm-Wine Drinkard* and between Adebisi and Odara in *The Brave African Huntress*. In each of these cases, the two parties to the duel are built up to such great heights that when the encounter finally takes place it assumes epic proportions.

Linked with this, is the author's high imaginative and descriptive power, applied often in character delineation. For example, one may forget many of the details of *Bush of Ghosts*, but certainly not the stationary monster, the Flash-eyed Mother, who instals herself "permanently" in the centre of the thirteenth town of ghosts. Apart from all other inconveniences, the inhabitants have the business of feeding the Flash-eyed Mother with her "millions of heads" and of enduring the cacophonous sound often made by these heads:

Millions of heads, which were just like a baby's head, appeared on her body, all circulated set by set. Each of these heads had two very short hands, which were used to hold their food or anything that they want to take, each of them had two eyes which were shining both day and night like fire-flies, one small mouth with numerous sharp teeth, the head was full of long dirty hair, two small ears like a rat's ears appeared on each side of the head. If they are talking, their voices would be sounding as if somebody strikes an iron or the church bell which sound would last more than ten minutes before stopping.[26]

The novels are full of highly descriptive passages, but not all are done on the elaborate scale of the Flash-eyed Mother. But even where the greatest economy of words is exercised, Tutuola still achieves a clear and effective image. In the following passage, one could almost hear the noise made by the skulls "rushing out" and "rolling on the ground". The effect is achieved by the apt comparison with "a thousand petrol drums" which itself contains an hyperbole:

But one day, the lady attempted to escape from the hole, and at the same time that the Skull who was watching her whistled to the rest of the Skulls that were in the backyard, the whole of them rushed out to the place where the lady sat on the bull-frog, so they caught her, but as all of them were rushing out, they were rolling on the ground as if a thousand petrol drums were pushing along a hard road.[27]

Other examples reveal that Tutuola has the eye for details and the power of observation which result in vivid description. His description of the "ultra-beautiful" ladies who are appointed watch-dogs over Simbi by the Satyr is attractive and meaningful in its context:

They were dressed in snow white attires which were full of the superfine decorations. The hairs on their heads were

---

[26] *Bush of Ghosts*, p. 98.
[27] *The Palm-Wine Drinkard*, p. 22.

glossy and were adorned with the decorations of gold flower, etc. which were glistening in the darkness. Everyone of them wore silver bead on neck, but Simbi was unable to describe the kind of the metal which they wore on their wrists, for all their snow white attires were sewn in long sleeves. All of them were neat and smart.[28]

So also is this description of the harmful creature which the Drinkard and his wife encounter in the Bush just before they reach Temites' House, particularly functional:

> He was white as if painted with white paint, he was white from foot to the topmost of his body, but he had no head or feet and hands like human-beings and he got one large eye on his topmost. He was long about ¼ of a mile and his diameter was about six feet, he resembled a white pillar.[29]

Another characteristic of Tutuola's writing is his use of conflicts, internal and external. These are of many kinds. There is the conflict of the kind which has already been mentioned — physical combat between two deadly enemies. There are also conflicts arising from the nature of the tasks the heroes have to perform, the encounters they have with their opponents and the steps they take to overcome obstacles in the way of their mission. Examples of these abound in each of the novels: the Drinkard has encounters, for instance, with bush animals, field creatures, 400 dead babies and with the hungry creature who, having eaten all that is available, still wants more. The boy-wanderer in *Bush of Ghosts,* has encounters with the golden, silverish and copperish ghosts, with the smelling ghosts, a spider-eating ghost and even with a talking piece of ground which refuses to be stepped upon by an "earthly person". "Don't smash me!" it says, "oh don't smash me, don't walk on me, go back to those who are chasing you to kill you, it is paining me too much as you are smashing me!"[30] Ajaiyi has encounters with the Spirit of Fire and the witch mother, not to mention his ordeal with the talking lump of iron. All these are in the area of external conflicts. These conflicts constitute an important centre of interest in

---
[28] *Simbi,* pp. 112—113.
[29] *The Palm-Wine Drinkard,* p. 42.
[30] *Bush of Ghosts,* p. 84.

Tutuola's novels. They provide the novels with activities and help to sustain the reader's interest to the end. In these novels, there are practically no dull moments. At any given time, the hero is either doing something or having something done to him or somebody else. Usually, what is being done is important or even crucial to the achievement of the hero's objective.

The internal conflicts are of a different order. They do not provide activities as such, but they often determine what activities are undertaken by the heroes. These conflicts result from some doubts and uncertainties in the minds of Tutuola's heroes, or their regrets as in the case of Simbi and the boy-wanderer in the *Bush of Ghosts* or their mental agony, as in the case of Ajaiyi. Simbi, who leaves home against the advice and better judgement of her mother, soon finds herself in trouble and this results in a state of mental conflict which manifests itself in frequent expressions of regret. "Hah; if I had obeyed my mother's warnings not to try to know the poverty and the punishment, all these should have not happened to me,"[31] she says in the town of the multi-coloured people after she has been made to undergo heavy punishment. This conflict is in Simbi all the time and it almost becomes a mental condition. The author makes it affect her actions and predetermine her reactions to situations in the novel. The same is true in *Ajaiyi*, where Ajaiyi and Aina are distressed because of their inherited poverty which only gets more chronic, the harder they work. Apart from physical strain, Ajaiyi suffers throughout from the thought of being a victim of natural injustice. This conflict provides the motivation of most of his actions in the novel.

Tutuola provides us in his novels with a world of dream visions, and, to enjoy him fully, one usually has to willingly suspend disbelief. It is only then, one can truly appreciate his magic world of dream-like fantasies with its ogres, monsters of every description and ghosts, a world where the living mingle freely with the dead but at their peril, a changeable world full of transformations. Critics have rightly called attention to this world of romance. But what is not always fully appreciated is, Tutuola's ability to blend realism with fantasy, with the result that in his type of world, we are sometimes relieved with touches of realism. *The Palm-Wine Drinkard* has many examples of these. Instead of providing himself magically

---

[31] *Simbi*, p. 61.

with everything he needs, as he may well have done, the Drinkard sometimes has to work hard like everybody else to get what he wants. Hence, he becomes a farmer on the Wraith Island and plants many kinds of crops. For using the land without the necessary permission, he gets into trouble with the animal-owner of the land. On another occasion when the Drinkard and his wife are beckoned by the Faithful-Hands to enter the White Tree, because of fear of the unknown, each of them wants the other to go in first. They continue to hesitate until they are both dragged in together by the Faithful-Hands. Before they finally get into the Tree, they conclude some business transaction to make provision for the future — "before we entered inside the white tree, we had 'sold our death' to somebody at the door for the sum of £70:18:6d and 'lent our fear' to somebody at the door as well on interest of £3:10:0d per month, so we did not care about death and we did not fear again."[32] At a stage in his journey, the Drinkard becomes "penniless" and decides on a brisk business: he converts himself into a canoe with which his wife ferries people across a river at the rate of three pence per adult and half fare for children. On the first day they make £7:5:3d and at the end of the month they have saved £56:11:9d. Again, when the Drinkard returns home with his magic egg, the greedy behaviour of the crowd at the scene of the food supplied by the egg is realistic, considering the fact that there has been a famine in the land for sometime and the people have been living at starvation level.

There are examples of realistic touches in the other novels as well. But only a few more need be given. Like the Drinkard and his wife, Simbi, in *Simbi* and Adebisi, in *The Brave African Huntress* at different stages on their journeys are compelled to work for their livelihood, Simbi in return for shelter provided by an old woman, Adebisi as an office servant. In *Bush of Ghosts*, the boy-wanderer and the Super Lady fall out because of disagreement over the upbringing of their son. In *Feather Woman*, the magic box which supplies the people with food to save them from starvation is stolen away by greedy night marauders. The suspicion with which the heroes are usually received in new communities is realistically motivated because in many cases they become the causes of great inconvenience and, in a few cases, agents of destruction to those

---

[32] *The Palm-Wine Drinkard*, p. 67.

communities the Drinkard brings about the destruction of the Red Town; Simbi disorganizes life in the Sinners' Town by beheading their king; Adebisi completely wipes out the pigmies; Ajaiyi, Ojo and Alabi inconvenienced everybody in the country of the witches with their talking lumps of iron. Such patches of realism in works, essentially conceived and executed in a spirit of fantasy, leave one with the impression that after all, Tutuola's world is not so naive and unreal. As Ronald Dathorne suggests, he is just as concerned with the problems of his society as any other writer: "Tutuola, better than any other writer in English-speaking Africa, has described the tensions of his society, its conflicts, its loyalties, the inner demands of a superstition that people cherish and the external demands of a materialism to which they must conform. This makes it creative literature."[33]

We see in these examples not only important aspects of Tutuola's narrative art, his method of bringing out the human significance of his works, but also the ways in which he expresses the link between tradition and modern experience by drawing freely from both. It is through the use of such techniques that he has succeeded in making his novels enduring works of arts.

---

[33] O. R. Dathorne, "The African Novel – Document to Experiment," *unpublished seminar paper* (1965), p. 7.

CHAPTER 3
THE NIGERIAN NOVEL AND THE PROBLEMS OF COMMUNICATION*

I.

In any serious consideration of the Nigerian Novel, one soon discovers how central an issue the problems of communication are. These problems are exhibited in two ways, mainly; the first, is the way the writer uses language, the second, is the way he presents those items he has selected for treatment. This article attempts to show how these problems affect our evaluation of the works of some Nigerian novelists. Examples are given of successful and unsuccessful Nigerian novelists with the aim of showing how crucial, effective communication is to the author and how a display of lack of creative intelligence often results in failure of communication.

Three novelists — Achebe, Egbuna and Okara — are discussed at some length. In each case, an attempt is made to examine closely the use of language by the novelist and to assess how effectively he communicates. From this examination, the successful artistry of Achebe and Okara becomes evident while with Egbuna, one finds several examples of failure to use language in the most imaginative manner.

II.

Achebe shows great skill in the art of communication. His works are of special significance to the investigator of the problems of communication, because he is interested in communication at all levels — between people of different cultures and religious beliefs, between people of the same race and political inclination, between different sections of the same community, between the Government and the people, between the town and country. This interest in communication is not altogether surprising for one, who has been a professional broadcaster. In all his novels, disaster results from

---

*This is an abridged version of a paper presented at the Commonwealth Literature Conference at Makerere, Uganda on 1 January, 1974, and published in *Lagos Review of English Studies* II edited by T. Vincent.

a breakdown in communication, either between two individuals as in *A Man of the People* or between an individual and his community as in *Things Fall Apart* and *Arrow of God*. The progressive deterioration in the quality of life, which one observes in Achebe's novels is caused, mainly by the appearance of an external influence or group which the people do not fully understand and therefore, cannot appreciate. His principal characters fail in all cases as a result of too much assertion of individualism. With Achebe, isolation spells disaster. His heroes come to grief as soon as they fail to communicate effectively with their people.

But communication is a two-way affair. Whenever it fails, usually the two sides in the system suffer as a result of the breakdown. That is why, the downfall of Achebe's heroes, usually, has a disastrous effect on the people. Although the heroes of *Things Fall Apart* and *Arrow of God* fall alone, their societies are never the same again after their exit. In *A Man of the People*, the society suffers just as much as its offending members. Even the fall of a weak character like Obi Okonkwo, leaves its mark in the fearful precedent it creates. To the extent that these heroes are embodiments of some of the weaknesses in society, their tragedy constitutes a sad commentary on society itself. This, in Achebe, is a sign that either or both of them have failed to communicate effectively. Achebe's greatness, therefore, must be seen in the way he balances the needs of the individual, against those of the society and the way he effectively utilizes the problems of communication to explore in depth the condition of man in society.

In *No Longer at Ease*, for example, Achebe presents a breakdown in communication at two levels: the personal level of Obe, who ends up isolated from all the groups and individuals with whom, he has had any kind of association — the European Club, the Umofia Progressive Union (U.P.U), his friends, Christopher and Joseph, and Clara — and the social group level between town and country. Obi makes an attempt to join the European Club, but soon finds that he cannot expect a solution to his problems from such a group. He, therefore, allows his membership of the Club to lapse, since, he has never at any time really considered himself a full member. It is only when his bid for social acceptance by the elements of modern life in the city has failed, that he makes any serious attempt at reconciliation with members of the U.P.U. Here, as elsewhere, Obi is destined to fail. It is usually through the use of language that Achebe isolates Obi from various groups in the novel. Obi either does not understand or appreciate the language of a group or is unable to make himself understood by its members.

Nothing brings out more clearly the social and cultural distance between country and town — and Obi's isolation from both — than the language employed by the author. Achebe usually succeeds in differentiating his characters through their speech. He requires this skill more here than in his first novel because here, he is dealing with two entirely different localities — Lagos and Umuofia. At each locality, there is need to differentiate between people at various stages of social development or levels of sophistication. In Lagos alone, there is.need to cope linguistically with the divergent groups represented by the U.P.U., the Club, Obi and his friends, Mr. Green and Miss Tomlinson, among others. The complex use of language in this novel is well illustrated by the situation, which arises when Obi is travelling from Lagos to Umuofia in public transport — the lorry driver speaks pidgin English to his passengers, the passengers sing in Igbo but Obi reflects on this song in English. Achebe handles this complicated linguistic situation skilfully and, on this as on other occasions, exposes Obi's isolation by way of calculated linguistic contrast:

> "Why you look the man for face when we want give um him two shillings?" he asked Obi.
> "Because he has no right to take two shillings from you," Obi answered.
> "Na him make I no de want carry you book people," he complained. "Too too know na him de worry una. Why you put your nose for matter way no concern you? Now that policeman go charge me like ten shillings."[1]

Obi, who speaks Standard English, is differentiated from the driver, who speaks pidgin English. But it is not only language that divides them. They are different in their moral orientation. Each language is made to denote a different scale of values and attitude to life. The driver sees nothing wrong in giving the traffic policeman a bribe of two shillings, while Obi considers it morally wrong to encourage bribery and corruption in this way. The driver's assessment of Obi — "Too too know na him de worry una!" — may appear to be

---

[1] Achebe, *No Longer at Ease*, African Writers Series Edition (London, 1969), p. 43. All page references are to this edition.

a hasty judgment in the circumstance, but it is significant in the way it points to the greatest flaw in Obi's character. It is the type of charge which might have been levelled against him by Joseph, Clara or any of the other characters from whom, he is now falling apart.

On many occasions, Achebe uses linguistic situations to highlight the differences between Obi and other groups. Consider, for example, the situation created at the reception organized by the U.P.U. Here is the pompous language of the Secretary in the address presented to Obi:

> Sir, we the officers and members of the above-named Union present with humility and gratitude this token of our appreciation of your unprecedented academic brilliance...
>
> He spoke of the great honour Obi had brought to the ancient town of Umuofia which could now join the comity of other towns in their march towards political irredentism, social equality and economic emancipation.
>
> The importance of having one of our sons in the vanguard of this march of progress is nothing short of axiomatic. Our people have a saying "Ours is ours, but mine is mine". Every town and village struggles at this momentous epoch in our political evolution to possess that of which it can say: "This is mine". We are happy that today we have such an invaluable possession in the person of our illustrious son and guest of honour.[2]

The author's intention here is clearly satirical. He uses a mocking tone to hold to ridicule a particular manner of using language. This is the language of a man, who wants to impress his semi-literate fellow-clansmen with his massive knowledge of English when, in fact, his control of the language is slight. Achebe immediately contrasts the Secretary's language with that of Obi, a graduate in English, who speaks simple and correct English — "is" and "was" — but whose English is considered "most unimpressive" by members of the Union.

On another occasion it is Obi, who experiences difficulty with language:

---

[2] *No Longer at Ease*, pp. 31–32.

He spoke about the wonderful welcome they had given him on his return. "If a man returns from a long journey and no one says 'nno' to him he feels like one who has not arrived". He tried to improvise a joke about beer and palm-wine, but it did not come off, and he hurried to the next point. He thanked them for the sacrifices they had made to send him to England. He would try his best to justify their confidence. The speech which had started off one hundred per cent in Igbo was now fifty-fifty.[3]

The linguistic situation described here shows how Obi, as a man of two worlds, is no longer at ease in either. The joke in Igbo about beer and palm-wine "did not come off", and this leads to a situation in which he becomes incoherent. He ends up speaking a hybrid language, half English, half-Igbo, truly symbolic of his own divided personality. As Mrs. Riddy points out,

... none of the languages available to him [Obi] is adequate to express the urban experience.

Furthermore, in this book languages are closely related to values; English and Ibo are not merely different ways of saying the same thing, but vehicles for expressing completely different attitudes to life. Where one language or the other proves inadequate, so for the same reasons do the values it represents.[4]

All languages prove inadequate to Obi. So he loses his sense of value and, with it, his identity.

III.

Just as Achebe's novels provide instances of effective communication, we have in the Nigerian novel several examples of failures of communication. The artistic fault in *Wind versus Polygamy*, for example, arises from the author's indulgence in overt documentary excessiveness to the detriment of a fully-realized relevant environ-

---

[3] *Ibid.*, p. 81.
[4] Felicity Riddy, "Language as a Theme in *No Longer at Ease*," *The Journal of Commonwealth Literature*, No. 9, (1970), pp. 38–39.

ment. Not only are the views of the various characters made explicit through a series of harangues, the characters themselves are portrayed in a way that lacks conviction:

> In our real African custom, marriage is only based on mature passionless analysis of two personalities. If they agree, they marry. If not, they don't. If a plant and a soil agree, the union produces good fruits. If not, it doesn't. African philosophy of marriage is based on thorough understanding of the laws of nature. Because we live with nature, we cannot divorce ourselves from the law of nature. That was why I said that our ancestors were the world's number one in the art of marriage. It is the duty of the present generation to export this profound timeless philosophy to the peoples in faraway places who are beyond the reach of the wave-lengths of nature's inspiration.[5]

Chief Ozuomba, the leading advocate of polygamy, proclaims his views on the subject in a pompous and illogical manner. The first sentence of the passage cannot stand without a great deal of qualification, and the analogy between the plant and soil is, at best, a specious one. "African philosophy of marriage is based on thorough understanding of the laws of nature", is a wild claim which cannot be justified on the grounds that Africans "live with nature". Living with nature does not make one's understanding of it necessarily "thorough". Ozuomba makes the unsupported claim of his ancestor's wide experience "in the art of marriage". Judged by the part he plays in the novel, the only inspiration he seems to have derived from the wisdom of his ancestors is to marry thirty-one wives. The novel deals in the main with the problems raised by his attempt to appropriate Elina, his thirty-second wife. This attempt constitutes an offence under the new Polygamy Act, which Ozuomba decides to fight. The novel, therefore, takes the form of a spirited defence of polygamy, led by Ozuomba.

But this defence is based, as we find in this passage, on dubious claims and false analogies, and is made in stilted language, particularly noticeable in the last sentence of the passage. Polygamy is referred to as "this profound timeless philosophy", which there is

---

[5] Obi Egbuna, *Wind versus Polygamy* (London, 1964), pp. 94–95. All page references are to this edition.

need "to export" to peoples "beyond the reach of the wave-lengths of nature's inspiration". The talk of exporting a philosophy and the use of words like "profound" and "wave-lengths" to discuss the domestic subject of polygamy show, the extent to which Ozuomba is meant to be unrealistic.

False claims and sheer verbiage characterize Ozuomba's speeches throughout the novel:

> For marriage to be a success, the partners must be like the poles of a magnet. When the north and south poles are brought together, they are bound to attract; you can never make two north poles attract, no matter how beautiful to the eye the shapes are or how physically close to each other you place them. It takes a physicist, or at any rate a man who knows the individual properties of the poles, to make the polar combination. In our old African societies, parents were such physicists. And wisely too. After all, parents are the encyclopaedia of their products. A well-paired marriage can never fail.[6]

The reader cannot but be alienated by the dogmatic manner in which the opinion in the first sentence is expressed and by the empty philosophising which pervades the whole piece. This is brought to its absurd climax in the identification of parents with physicists and the reference to them as "encyclopaedia". The word "never" in the last sentences makes the whole statement unacceptable and shows how inflexibly Ozuomba's opinions are expressed.

Egbuna's method of satire is to get Ozuomba, "the Black Solomon", to "discuss with astonishing profundity"[7] many aspects of the suject of polygamy which are clearly beyond his comprehension. His opinion here on a highly controversial subject is a case in point:

> There is no such thing as the equality of the sexes. Either the man stays on top and plays the man. Or the woman stays on top and dictates to the man. The woman is more ruthless when she has the least opportunity of power. In the West, she has created the myth of gentlemanliness to achieve her

---

[6] *Wind versus Polygamy*, p. 95.
[7] *Ibid.*, p. 33.

purpose. A gentleman must, like a house-boy surrender his seat to a lady. He must not argue with a lady. He must, like a school-boy before his head teacher, doff his hat to a lady. He must surrender his salary to his wife and queue with his own son every week for pocket-money. He bows when the lady genuflects. To qualify for a lover, he must drink wine from the shoe of a lady.[8]

The first sentence leads one to expect a reasoned argument against the equality of the sexes. This hope is immediately dashed. What follows is a series of exaggerations and a false picture of life, which confirm the extreme naivety of the speaker. The fact that this is advanced as part of a serious defence of polygamy, which has many convincing points in its favour, makes it all the more absurd. Considering the setting for this speech, the City High Court, it is highly unlikely that anybody present would believe, for example, that, to qualify for a lover, a man "must drink wine from the shoe of a lady". In his attempt to impress others with his extensive knowledge of life in the West, Ozuomba only succeeds in making himself an object of ridicule.

In the conflict between the old and the new, between tradition and modernism, the old, as represented by Ozuomba and others, is presented as inadequate. But so also are the modern ideas which Ogidi, Jerome and Elina symbolize. Ogidi deserves to fail in his bid for Elina, who later falls in love with, and finally marries Jerome. But the love affair between the two is so maladroitly handled that Jerome's achievement means little to the reader. The novelist devotes the whole of chapter four to a love scene between the two, but his treatment of this situation which calls for the use of imagination is highly unimaginative:

> "Thank God you are here at last, Eliṇa".
> "Oh Jeromy!" whispered Elina in return.
> "Thank God too that you waited. Knowing your temper as I do, I was ever so afraid you might think I've let you down and go away in anger."
> "Every minute I waited was like an eternity, believe me..."
> "I am sorry, Jeromy."

---

[8] *Ibid.*, p. 98.

"But then, your being here has transformed every eternity into a fraction of a second."[9]

This is how the young lovers start their meeting in "a lonely wood". They employ the stale language of a tired romanticism and address each other in cliches — "Every minute I waited was like eternity", "Your being here has transformed every eternity into a fraction of a second". These expressions are ultimately meaningless and succeed only in making this moonlight picnic totally unreal. And consider the following:

> You forced my father into nothing. Get that into your head, Elina. As far as he is concerned, you could be just any woman. My father sees you just as a number in the family register. To me, you are much more than a number. You are a figure.
> "A figure?" said Elina in bewilderment. "But a figure is only a part of a number. A part can't be greater than a whole."
> "In commercial arithmetic, yes. In arithmetic of hearts, it is the reverse."[10]

Here the conversation verges on the absolutely idiotic in the ridiculous attempt to establish a connection between "commercial arithmetic" and "arithmetic of hearts". But the worst is yet to be. After a long spell, during which more inane words are spoken, the dialogue continues:

> "Are you really having a wonderful time, Elina?"
> "Yes, Jeromy. So wonderful it frightens me. I've never felt like this about any other man in my life. What do you think it is, Jeromy?"
> "I can't be quite sure of my diagnosis till I've made one final test," Jerome replied, grinning with a mischievous expression he undoubtedly inherited or copied from his father.
> "What kind of test is that?" Elina asked in all innocence.
> "Oh, a simple test, really. The aim of the experiment is

---

[9] *Ibid.*, p. 76.
[10] *Ibid.*, p. 77.

to measure the frequency of our heart-beats when our lips
are pressed together. These palpitations are caused by a flow
of a special type of inter-lipial current which incidentally can
only pass between people diametrically poled. In unacademic
circles, I believe they call it — kissing."
Elina blushed, turned and tried to change the subject.[11]

The passage lacks anything one can credibly associate with the speeches of young people genuinely in love with each other. Jerome's "experiment" is described in a language devoid of sincerity and therefore, incapable of exciting any sympathetic response from Elina. There is a blatant case of artistic failure here. Since the love affair between these two is meant to succeed, why, one might ask, is it presented in a way that bores rather than interests the reader? There is no full realization of the background against which monogamy is being considered, or any dramatization of the social and cultural conditions, in which the type of monogamous connection contemplated by Jerome and Elina might succeed or fail. If both the past and present are inadequate, surely a way must lie forward to the future if a social vacuum is to be avoided. This way is indicated in the type of relationship which has developed between Jerome and Elina. What has obscured this vision is the novelist's inadequate presentation of the relationship. This aspect of the work shows Egbuna as an author of very limited competence. Professor Dathorne must have had this weakness and the novelist's addiction to overt statements in mind when he wrote about the novel:

> This is the worst African novel I have ever read. It is the
> story of Elina and her problems of love and might have done
> well in the Onitsha series.[12]

The phrase, "the Onitsha series", is, of course, used here in a pejorative sense. Even so, the comment does Egbuna only little injustice. An important consideration is his overall poor performance in this novel, especially the extent to which the love scene between Jerome and Elina is inefficiently handled.

---

[11] *Ibid.*, pp. 78—79.
[12] O. R. Dathorne, A Review in *Black Orpheus*, 17 (1965), p. 59.

IV.

On the other hand, one cannot but be favourably impressed by the symbolic manner in which Okara communicates in *The Voice*.[13] Okara's prose style is so unique and contributes so significantly to the success of the novel that it deserves detailed consideration. We are told by the novelist himself that his style is influenced by Ijaw way of thinking and that his principal aim in all his writings is," to capture the living images of African speech".[14] But to call his style "experimental", as Professor Roscoe does in his book, is to suggest that it is capable of improvement, modification and possible future use.[15] I believe that Okara's adopted prose style has grown out of the artistic necessities of *The Voice* and represents the kind of achievement which cannot endure repetition. Okolo means "voice"; in this case, the voice of wisdom, "the voice of vision". Okara's strange English prose is his peculiar invention in which his hero expresses his "voice", his self-identity, declares his total awareness of human experience and defines his relationship with a changing world. Again, since Okolo in his social and moral orientation is different from the other villagers, there is need for him to emphasize this difference in his "spoken words", which are the weapons of ultimate victory. This is the rationale for Okara's language, the circumstances which justify his unusual English syntax. I regard the symbolic language of *The Voice*, as an integral part of what is created and one which cannot be separated from the total meaning and the universal message of the novel.

Contrary to what Okara's declared intention would lead one to expect and the impression given by a number of critics, Okara's prose style is not entirely dominated by the linguistic characteristics of his native Ijaw.[16] His language is, in fact, a compound of many simples. The Ijaw influence is no doubt important but there are other influences as well, providing linguistic features different from those of Ijaw. Whichever features are most noticeable at any particular time depends on the developing situation:

---

[13] Gabriel Okara, *The Voice*, African Writers Series, (London, 1970). All page references are to this edition.
[14] G. Okara, "African Speech... English words," *Transition*, Vol. 3, No. 10, (1963).
[15] Roscoe, *Mother is Gold* (London, 1971), pp. 113–121.
[16] See, for example, Margaret Laurence, *Long Drums and Cannons* (London, 1968), pp. 196–8; Ann Tibble, *African/English Literature* (London, 1965), pp. 81–92.

Third messenger: "Your nonsense words stop. These things have meaning no more. So stop talking words that create nothing..."
First messenger: "Listen not to him. He speaks this way always because he passed standard six. Because he passed standard six his ears refuseth nothing, his inside refuseth nothing like a dustbin..."
Third messenger (Angrily): "Shut your mouth. You know nothing."
First messenger (Also angrily): "Me know nothing? Me know nothing? Because I went not to school I have no bile, I have no head? Me know nothing? Then answer me this. Your hair was black black be, then it became white like a white cloth and now it is black black be more than blackness."[17]

Many of the features of Okara's prose style are present here. The Ijaw influence is noticeable in sentences like "I have no bile, I have no head?" and the inverted command: "Your nonsense words stop." The Ijaw method of simple repetition for emphasis is responsible for "black black" (Standard English: very black) and the modified form "white like a white cloth", "black black be more than blackness". This method of emphasis is used throughout the novel:

You have been silent more than silence.[18]
He... came and sat near Okolo with smile smile in his mouth.[19]
On this cold cold ground we have been walking.[20]
Whatever they do to Okolo is nothing nothing.[21]

But other influences, apart from those of Ijaw, are discernible from the passage. The whole of the first speech of the first messenger is in the type of Standard English appropriate to his status except for the use of the biblical ending "eth" in "refuseth". "Shut your mouth. You know nothing... Me know nothing?" is pidgin English,

---
[17] *The Voice*, pp. 24–25.
[18] *Ibid.*, p. 65.
[19] *Ibid.*, p. 83.
[20] *Ibid.*, p. 91.
[21] *Ibid.*, p. 97.

which may well be used by messengers in these circumstances. Even a short statement like "He will come. He worked overtime. Let us wait small",[22] has the first two sentences in Standard English and the last in pidgin English.

When there is need for speed in the action of the novel, Okara often reflects this need by abandoning his adopted prose style and writing in Standard English:

> When day broke the following day it broke on a canoe aimlessly floating down the river. And in the canoe tied together back to back with their feet tied to the seats of the canoe, were Okolo and Tuere. Down they floated from one bank of the river to the other like debris, carried by the current. Then the canoe was drawn into a whirlpool. It spun round and round and was slowly drawn into the core and finally disappeared. And the water rolled over the top and the river flowed smoothly over it as if nothing had happened.[23]

"Then the canoe was drawn into a whirlpool" is particularly significant. It shows Okara's growing fascination with an idea which provides the objective for all his works. "I think the immediate aim of African writing," he once declared, "is to put into the whirlpool of literature the African point of view".[24] Here the hero is submerged in a whirlpool and, with him, the noble ideals for which he stands. Since, we are already told that his spoken words "will not die", this manner of death is a symbolic way of assuring us of his re-appearance in a new and more hopeful form.

Okara's ability to regulate his speed of narration according to the requirements of art, is particularly attractive in the way it frequently enables the reader to assimilate gradually the numerous details necessary for a correct assessment of the work:

> The people snapped at him like hungry dogs snapping at bones. They carried him in silence like the silence of ants carrying a crumb of yam or fish bone. Then they put him down and dragged him past thatch houses that in the dark looked like pigs with their snouts in the ground; pushed

---
[22] *Ibid.*, p. 107.
[23] *Ibid.*, p. 127.
[24] *Cultural Events in Africa,* No. 102 (undated), p. 4.

and dragged him past mud walls with pitying eyes; pushed
and dragged him past concrete walls with concrete eyes;
pushed and dragged him along the waterside like soldier ants
with their prisoner. They pushed and dragged him in panting
silence, shuffling silence, broken only by an owl hooting from
the darkness of the orange tree.[25]

The brisk movement of the first two sentences reflects the swiftness of the initial actions of the people. But later on, by means of repetitions, and the jerky movement which results from them, we are made to feel the cumulative effect of "pushed and dragged", and, to that extent, the difficulty of the hero who suffers in silence. The hooting of the owl underlines the gravity of the situation.

An entirely different kind of impression is given by a passage like this, also written in Standard English:

"You speak English, of course?"
"Yes," answered Okolo.
"You want to see the Big One?"
"Yes!"
"What about?"
"I want to ask him if he's got it."
"Have you ever heard of the word psychiatrist?"
"Yes."
"Do you know what a psychiatrist does?"
"Yes."
"Have you consulted one?"
"No."[26]

Okolo and the white police chief have little in common and would be glad to be rid of each other quickly. This impatience is reflected in the dialogue, especially in Okolo's short answers. On the other hand, a character like Tuere communicates mainly in symbols and takes all the time she needs to make her point:

Don't you see it in your inside that when everybody raises
his hand for you and sings your praise in song, you are turning

---

[25] *The Voice*, pp. 38–39.
[26] *Ibid.*, p. 86.

the insides of the people against them? So you were a big tree fallen across their path. They could not move it or cut it as they did me because you have been to school. And so they had to cut a path around it by passing the word round that your head is not correct.[27]

Okara is remarkably successful in achieving the various levels of speech appropriate to character and situations, and in adapting the relevant features of his adopted prose style to different circumstances. Those critics, like Eldred Jones and Ronald Dathorne, who dismiss Okara's prose style lightly do not seem to have given sufficient consideration to its many features and the various aspects of its use in the novel.[28] His style, especially in those sections dominated by Ijaw syntax and way of thinking, has the overall effect of slowing down the action and inducing a quality of contemplation which fits the theme of the novel:

> It was the day's ending and Okolo by a window stood. Okolo stood looking at the sun behind the tree tops falling. The river was flowing, reflecting the finishing sun, like a dying away memory. It was like an idol's face, no one knowing what is behind. Okolo at the palm trees looked. They were like women with hair hanging down, dancing, possessed. Egrets, like white flower petals strung slackly across the river, swaying up and down, were returning home. And, on the river, canoes were crawling home with bent backs and tired hands, paddling.[29]

Here we see the dramatic effect of Okara's prose as it rises to fine poetic heights. By placing his verbs close to the end of the sentence, the novelist is no doubt reproducing the Ijaw sentence structure of subject-object-verb. This gives the prose a sense of cadence and provides an appropriate setting for "the day's ending", with the various objects either coming to rest or withering away. "The finishing sun", "dying away memory", "canoes were crawling home

---

[27] *Ibid.*, p. 55.
[28] Eldred Jones, "Locale and Universe: Three Nigerian Novels," *Journal of Commonwealth Literature*, No. 3 (1967), p. 129; Ronald Dathorne, "The African Novel – Document to Experiment" (Unpublished Manuscript), p. 11.
[29] *The Voice*, p. 26.

Ijaw idiom and word order into English. The motivating force is undoubtedly his determination to devise consciously an English prose style, influenced by Ijaw and other factors, suitable for his creative purpose in *The Voice*.

V.

The attempt to project Nigerian culture, past and present, and describe the realities and conflicts of modern life in the Nigerian novel, poses many problems of communication which each author has tried to solve in his particular way. The most attractive solutions are provided in the realistic manner, in which novelists like Achebe and Okara tackle the problems of communication which arise in their works. These novelists intelligently adapt the English Language to the need for presenting a rural culture and of criticizing traditional life at the literal and symbolic levels. Okara's use of symbols to perform essential linguistic functions, introduces an exciting new dimension to the Nigerian novel. It is through the use of concrete images that Okara offers us glimpses into the inner life and experiences of his hero and other characters. It is also in a symbolic manner that he presents the vision of hope, the ultimate triumph of truth over falsehood, which is the universal message of *The Voice*. Again, it is his use of symbolic language that enables Okara to draw Izongo and Okolo in moral contrast to each other and, in the process, to demonstrate his very critical attitude towards the traditional elements in contemporary society. The unique achievement of successful Nigerian novelists like Achebe and Okara has been made possible by their incisive analysis and evaluation of character and conduct, presented in an exciting narrative capable of stimulating the sympathetic response of the reader.

CHAPTER 4
THE LINK BETWEEN TRADITION AND MODERN EXPERIENCE IN THE NIGERIAN NOVEL*

I.

Nigerian novelists, like other writers, have been influenced by their environment and the circumstances in history which helped to make that environment what it is today. They write partly to explain the social dilemma of the group to which they belong and partly to portray a way of life which might have survived — and to some extent has survived — if certain historical events had not so drastically affected Africa and the attitude of Africans not only to people of other races but also to their own selves.

Therefore, no Nigerian novelist is not in one way or another, and sometimes in several ways at once, preoccupied with his country's indigenous culture. From author to author, however, the directions and emphases which this preoccupation involves vary in important respects. To put it for the time being rather roughly and crudely, one has something like, near uncritical total acceptance at one end of the scale, and decidedly critical scrutiny at the other. It is with the problems of communicating to the reader just what his sense of the place and value of Nigerian indigenous culture is, that this approach to the Nigerian novelist will be concerned. Two questions will be constantly kept in mind:

(a) What is the attitude (or what are perhaps the several attitudes) of novelist X towards his country's culture?
(b) What type of link does the novelist establish between tradition and modern life?

In a short article of this kind, only a few works can be discussed in any detail. There is no attempt here at a comprehensive survey of all the novels available. But enough will be said in each case, to indicate the artistic use a writer has made of Nigerian culture in his imaginative scheme.

---

*First published in *Studies in Black Literature* V/3, 1974, pp. 11–16.

II.

Of all the novelists discussed in this article, Amos Tutuola stands closest to first sources, to the roots of oral tradition. His six novels draw freely on Yoruba folklore, his main source, and his attitude to the culture which produced it is one of near uncritical total acceptance. These novels are written in English but it is a type of English which represents a bodily translation from Yoruba, Tutuola's first language, in which he probably does all his thinking.[1] This peculiar use of English, considered unacceptable or even offensive by some Nigerians, has helped to ensure a predominant oral tone and reinforce the cultural value of his works. His novels are no doubt rooted in Yoruba tradition, but his achievement as a writer, lies in the way he has extended the traditional fantasy in the Yoruba folktales, to cover aspects of modern life and industrial civilization while at the same time reminding people in contemporary life of the values and conditions of their ancestral past.

It is interesting to compare Tutuola's attitude to Yoruba culture in his works with Tafawa Balewa's attitude to Hausa culture and Islam in *Shaihu Umar*.[2] In a way, the story of *Shaihu Umar* is like any of Tutuola's, especially *Bush of Ghosts*, deprived of its dream visions, monsters and ghosts. As with the boy-wanderer in Bush of Ghosts, the suffering of *Shaihu Umar* is real. Each returns to his country at the end of his journey and experiences a wiser man. Furthermore, the adventures of Umar's mother, when she sets out to look for her kidnapped child, take the quest pattern. In her case, as with all of Tutuola's heroes and heroines, many obstacles are interposed between her and the object of her quest in order to make the task difficult to accomplish. Her ill-treatment at the hands of Ago and the Tripoli slave dealer, Ahmad, is one of such obstacles. As is the case with Tutuola, what Balewa has done is to refurbish an

---

[1] Between 1952 and 1967 Tutuola wrote the following novels, all published by Faber and Faber, London.
   The Palm-Wine Drinkard, 1952
   My Life in the Bush of Ghosts, 1954.
   Simbi and the Satyr of the Dark Jungle, 1955. (*Simbi*)
   The Brave African Huntress, 1958.
   Feather Woman of the Jungle, 1962.
   Ajaiyi and His Inherited Poverty. 1967.
[2] Page references are to Tafawa Balewa, *Shaihu Umar*, translated by Mervyn Hiskett (London, 1968).

old tale by employing well-known motifs and narrative techniques, thus giving a new depth and a different dimension to what might have been an ordinary story.

But there are also differences, which are far more significant than the similarities. While Tutuola is immersed in the cultural consciousness of Yoruba traditions, as embodied in cosmology, moral values and attitudes, Balewa derives his inspiration from history and Islam. Again, while in the Tutuola novel, the withdrawal or transposition of incidents, especially those in the middle, is usually of little structural consequence, the organization of *Shaihu Umar* is such that the withdrawal of any incidents would undermine the quality of the experience provided by the novelist. *Shaihu Umar* utilizes history to present an imaginative reconstruction of events. It is a story of intense, and at times alarming, individual experience which relies for its success on the devices of traditional verbal art, especially the simple speech rhythms of the story-teller. The story-telling session takes place with *Umar* sitting in the midst of his students, in the evening, anxious to instruct them. A high degree of motivation is provided by the question of an eager student. The conditions are therefore, established for an important social experience, and all the essentials of a successful story-telling event are present.[3] Because of their common interest, rapport is achieved between *Umar* and his audience, and this generates continuous perceptual responses which are interpreted by both sides as feedback. As the story progresses, we find that the listeners continually try to decode what the story-teller has encoded. The tension building up within the message as a result of this story-teller-listener interaction, reaches its peak in the adoration of *Umar* — "Certainly this is no mere man, he is a saint."[4]

An attractive feature of Balewa's writing, which is apparent even in translation, is his economy of style. But a direct and economical style is only one of the achievements of *Shaihu Umar*. Its real value lies in the light it throws on Hausa life and culture at the end of the last century, especially on the impact of the slave trade and Islam on the society. For example, the bitter experiences of *Umar's* mother as the domestic slave of Ahmad, are used to illustrate

---

[3] For a set of postulates on story transmission see, for example, Robert A. Georges, "Toward an Understanding of Storytelling Events," *Journal of American Folklore*, Vol. 82, No. 326 (1969), pp. 313–28.
[4] *Shaihu Umar*, p. 18.

the conditions of life at the time:

> He had her put in chains. All the hardest housework, she had to do it, and she was only given food at irregular intervals. For her part, because of her unhappiness and brooding on her misfortunes, she became completely worn out, and she lost her good looks. When she finished work, she would just sit down and weep.
> When he saw this, he said to himself. "This slave is thoroughly disobedient, and beating is the only cure for it". Time and again he beat her, but despite this she did not change her attitude. He went on punishing her in this way for about a year. But for her part, all this hardship that she suffered did not trouble her, for what always lay heavy on her mind was her failure to find her son.[5]

She gets into this pathetic situation when she goes in search of her son who himself has been snatched away in a raid. Her only opportunity of becoming free through the intervention of a cadi is lost. By making both mother and son victims of the traffic in human beings, the novelist emphasizes the insecurity to life which is an essential part of the slave trade. But this is done in a manner which must appear to most readers curiously detached — the slave raider shows no remorse, the slave no self-pity. All we are told is: "for her part, all this hardship that she suffered did not trouble her."

It is typical of this author that nowhere in this novel, does he display any moral indignation against a system as iniquitous as the slave trade. One might suspect that he has done this in order to show his approval of the teaching of Islam which permits slavery. Or is he merely anxious to demonstrate that the realistic acceptance of things as they are is an important feature of the Hausa character? Whatever the reason, the portrait we have of *Umar's* mother — her simple piety and unlimited patience, her consideration for others and her preparedness to risk her life for the sake of her son — represents a Hausa ideal of womanhood. This picture is only partly redeemed by realistic descriptions which show her capable of ordinary human emotions and weaknesses — "When she finished

---

[5] *Ibid.*, p. 69.

work she would just sit down and weep." The author's attitude of tolerance is also reflected in the discipline he imposes on his prose. In this passage, for example, he avoids the use of highly emotive words in a situation that admits of some display of emotion. Nor is there any striving after literary effects. Even so, almost effortlessly, he succeeds in conveying to the reader the hardship suffered by *Umar's* mother and her resignation to her fate.

The novel regards Islam not only as a religion but also as a way of life. It is the source of the hero's inner strength from which springs his determination to live down the cruelty of the days of slavery and establish himself as a Muslim scholar. Balewa, himself a one-time Education Officer, writing with an intimate knowledge of the traditional system of Muslim education and the eagerness of the people for knowledge of the Koran, endows his hero with all the learning and piety of a Muslim divine:

> In this little town there was once a certain malam, learned in the stars, in the Koran, and in the scriptures, and an upholder of the Faith. This malam was one of the men of this world to whom God has given the gift of knowledge.
> ... So great were his learning and wisdom that news of him reached countries far distant from where he lived. Men would come from other countries, travelling to him in order to seek knowledge.[6]

Balewa presents Islam with great tenderness and admiration as the religion which has exercised a profound influence on the evolution of Hausa Society. The effect of its teaching as regards predestination and submission to the will of God, reveals itself in the way the characters in this novel submit to their environment without any conscious attempt to influence or change it. One can therefore conclude that, although in *Shaihu Umar*, Balewa is critical of certain aspects of life, like the intrigues at court and the evils of the slave trade, his main interest appears to have been to use the story form to describe the moral and social conditions, in which his characters live with an implication of what is on the whole, a mild criticism of society.

---

[6] *Ibid.*, p. 18.

III.

The process started by Tutuola is carried so much further by Achebe, that it may be difficult at first to appreciate the connection between the two. In fact, both novelists rely heavily on traditional lore and indigenous customs and write with a distinctly sociological bias. Each has created in his own time literary structures in which he gives expression to authentic Nigerian experiences and has relied, to varying degrees, on the resources of his first language. Both novelists, therefore, exhibit in their writings features which may be described as uniquely Nigerian. What, in the main, differentiates Achebe from Tutuola is that, in Achebe, the criticism of past and present Nigerian societies, particularly Igbo society, is more pungent and the link between the past and present, much stronger. This is achieved by the way Achebe presents the traditional customs and practices of his people in situations which suggest the deep convictions of the characters, who believed in them, and in his use of an English-language diction appropriate to character, theme and situation.[7] Tutuola makes no conscious attempt to do the first and succeeds, only partially, in his last novel with the second.

Another reason for Achebe's success is his ability to look at a situation from very varied points of view, sometimes bringing them before the reader simultaneously. The reader finds, almost invariably, that no one point of view is wholly acceptable and that, to reach a satisfying conclusion, several points of view have to be taken into consideration. This quality is owed to Achebe's successful attempt to present many sides of a case with apparent impartiality. For example, he does not seek to explain, justify or condemn the Igbo background against which he mostly writes. He no doubt has a great admiration for this life, but he does not idealize it nor does he at any stage become sentimental in his presentation. Beside the strengths, he gives weaknesses in tribal society. We therefore, have a true and complete picture in which the whole of the background is fully realized. We are given enough information about the people, for us to feel well acquainted with them and their

---

[7] Page references are to the following African Writers series editions of the novels:
  Things Fall Apart (London, 1969).
  No Longer at Ease (London, 1969).
  Arrow of God (London, 1967).
  A Man of the People (London, 1969).

way of life. We have realistically and convincingly presented many aspects of village life — the feast of the New Yam, the wrestling contest at the "ilo", the display of the "egwugwu" on festive occasions, the religious beliefs and activities of the people, their desire for health, happiness and success in life, their attitude to war and their devotion to farming, which is their main occupation, to mention only a few. In the opinion of Professor Walsh:

> Whether the vision of Ibo society given in the novels is justified by history is almost irrelevant. What we have in this work is a conception of civilisation which has a root in reality. It includes a world and a group with a coherent anatomy of standards and beliefs and a solid convincing body. This is a universe perfectly suited to a novelist. It is complete but small. It incorporates a standard and it expresses itself in a characteristic mode of living...[8]

But the weaknesses are there and Achebe does not attempt to conceal them. We see in these people, an attitude of intolerance towards strangers and outside influence. They are suspicious of everything new. The fear of some unknown evil which may afflict them at any time seems to dominate their lives:

> Darkness held a vague terror for these people, even the bravest among them. Children were warned not to whistle at night for fear of evil spirits. Dangerous animals became even more sinister and uncanny in the dark. A snake was never called by its name at night, because it would hear. It was called a string.[9]

Individuals seem to be perpetually on their guard, lest they unwittingly bring some misfortune upon themselves or the tribe as a whole:

> "Ekwefi!" a voice called from one of the other huts. It was Nwoye's mother, Okonkwo's first wife.
> "Is that me?" Ekwefi called back. That was the way

---

[8] William Walsh, *A Manifold Voice* (London, 1970), p. 50.
[9] *Things Fall Apart*, p. 9.

> people answered calls from outside. They never answered yes for fear it might be an evil spirit calling.[10]

This element of fear turns out to be important in the development of Achebe's novels. First, it explains the society's rejection of anything which looks abnormal, like albinos and twins. Secondly, it helps to ensure that any strangers, who attempt to establish themselves in this society in the name of religion or good government will be resisted. So we find that, although the society has a concreteness of its own, it is not designed for dynamic growth. Even without much external pressure, a society which barricades itself against new ideas and forms of action is likely to experience a moral decline, not to mention an economic one. The process of disintegration is accelerated by the arrival of new groups with new ideas which are at first totally incomprehensible to the people. In this way, the society pays a high price for its inflexibility, its inability to make necessary adjustment with time, its incapacity for change.

Another result of this attitude of mind is the mutual suspicion and tension it generates among the people themselves. The distrust of outsiders is soon directed inwards to the society. The result is that the people do not trust one another to the extent one would expect in such a closely-knit tribal society:

> We grew up knowing that the world was full of enemies. Our father had protective medicine located at crucial points in our house and compound. One, I remember, hung over the main entrance; but the biggest was in a gourd in a corner of his bedroom. No child went alone into that room which was virtually always under lock and key anyway. We were told that such and such homes were never to be entered; and those people were pointed out to us from whom we must not accept food.[11]

This inclination to distrust, Achebe uses for his artistic purpose. His novels record the stresses and tensions in society. Some of these merely provide the necessary motivation for action, while others

---

[10] ibid., pp. 37–38.
[11] *A Man of the People*, pp. 32–33.

are developed into full-scale rivalries between diametrically-opposed religious or political groups. So, although Achebe's attitude to Igbo culture is one of calculated respect, he shows intelligent objectivity in his presentation of Igbo life and character.

IV.

In Nigerian novels, the link between tradition and modern experience is usually presented in a way which implies criticism of both the past and present. *Wind versus Polygamy*, for example, is an apparent defence of polygamy.[12] But this defence is carried out so energetically, and in such circumstances, that the reader soon discovers that the author's aim is, in fact, to ridicule the idea. But the alternative system, monogamy, is also satirized. In Nwankwo's novel, Danda represents the dilemma of many of Aniocha man.[13] He is enticed by the dancing and feasting of pagan life; yet, he is attracted by the claims to modernity which many believe can only be fully satisfied if one embraces Christianity. The two positions are made mutually exclusive, and this results in tension for the individual and the society. This tension is described in a way which exposes the inadequacy of both paganism and Christianity. In whichever novel we turn to, we find the past and present satirized. A feeling of disappointment is everywhere in evidence. But while authors like Egbuna and Adaora Ulasi, are content merely to present this feeling, Nwankwo provides the reader with a more exciting experience in the way, he skilfully describes the tensions underlying the apparently smooth surface of accepted corporate life and the attempt of the individual to break through. The greater sophistication of *The Voice* is indicated in the manner Okara presents his total rejection of society and projects his vision of the future, all in a symbolic language which adopts the same transliterative device which he has used successfully in his poems.[14] It is necessary to discuss a few novels in some detail to see how individual writers have exhibited their sense of disappointment with the past and present.

For example, Adaora Ulasi in *Many Thing You No Understand* is

---

[12] Obi Egbuna, *Wind versus Polygamy* (London, 1964).
[13] Nkem Nwankwo, *Danda* (London, 1970).
[14] Gabriel Okara, *The Voice* (London, 1970).

concerned with the inadequacy of the old and the new.[15] Her novel presents a confrontation between a colonial authority represented by Mason, the District Officer, and MacIntosh, the Assistant District Officer, and the traditional authority of Ukana, represented by Obieze III and the village elders, Okafor and Chukwuka, on the obnoxious practice of burying several human heads with a dead Chief. Because of the demands of tradition, a criminal offence is committed. Each of the expatriate officers tackles the problem in the way that seems to him best and each is worsted and humiliated in turn. On the face of it then, tradition triumphs. But at what price? Victory for tradition is achieved in particular cases either by a mean exploitation of group loyalty, which prevents offenders like Okafor and Chukwuka from being apprehended by the law, or by an unconvincing application of magic, similar to the use of "iyi ocha" in *Wand of Noble Wood*. In order to prove to the expatriate officers that there are "many thing you no understand here.... I no think say you go fit understand them for long, long time"[16] MacIntosh is made insane and Mason is ambushed and disgraced. By these events, as with the disappearance of the District Officer in Miss Ulasi's second novel, the villagers intend to show their strength and unity of purpose.[17]

But with these activities, come the systematic erosion of traditional authority:

> Chief Obieze, I no like for stay for fortress. And if A.D.O. stay here for Ukana he go catch me one day. I no know about Okafor. But for my own self I know say I no fit hide for fortress like animal him hunter look for, for the rest of my life! Fortress tire me. I no have woman for three day. I be married man with plenty wife and I live inside there like man who no get wife![18]

Leaders of the community suffer as much as the expatriate officers. The experiences of Chukwuka and Okafor, in the fortress are unpleasant, but they strike the reader as an inadequate punishment for the trouble they bring on the community as a whole by their actions.

---

[15] Page references are to Adaora Ulasi, *Many Thing You No Understand*, (London, 1970).
[16] *Many Thing You No Understand*, p. 188.
[17] See Adaora Ulasi, *Many Thing Begin for Change* (London, 1971).
[18] *Many Thing You No Understand*, p. 147.

The Link Between Tradition and Modern Experience in the Nigerian Novel 57

These leaders are in the end, discredited and Chief Obieze's reputation is tarnished by the support he gives to criminals against innocent citizens. The picture of Ukana, is that, of a community where the people's inclusive togetherness and obscurantist attitudes result in injustice and block social progress. Where each side to an encounter comes in for a measure of satire, no side can claim absolute victory over the other. In the clash between tradition and modernism, as described in this novel, neither side appears sufficiently well-equipped to emerge unscathed.

Adaora Ulasi dramatizes very effectively, the breakdown in communication between the two sides:

> "Mr. Mbaezue, you're on a charge of attempted murder. We all know that you were provoked, but there it is. Finding another man with your wife doesn't justify you attempting to kill him."
> "The A.D.O. said, killing people is very bad."
> "Do you plead guilty or not guilty?"
> "He said, you sin or you not sin?"
> The accused again addressed himself to the interpreter.
> "Mr. Mbaezue said, he not guilty."
> "You tried to take a man's life, Mbaezue. It's attempted murder. It's up to the court, though, to take into consideration the reason that motivated you, and perhaps be lenient. I find you guilty of attempted manslaughter. I sentence you to five years hard labour."
> "He said, you sin. You go for jail for five year."
> Mbaezue shook his head and mumbled: "Appeal."[19]

Apart from the power of "juju" and the fierce loyalty to tradition and community, one other aspect of Ukana life which the expatriate officers get to know is its criminality. Each court case provides the novelist an opportunity to expose a member of the community to ridicule for some serious offence. Humour in this case results from the difference in quality between the opinion expressed by the Assistant District Officer and what the interpreter says. There is a vast difference, for example, between "The A.D.O. said, killing people is very bad" and what the Officer actually says — the whole

---

[19] *ibid.*, pp. 8–9.

of the first paragraph of the passage. Since most of what the A.D.O. says, especially the reasoning on which he bases his final judgement, is lost in translation, the reader is not surprised that Mbaezue finds the verdict of the court unacceptable and decides to challenge it. In this, as in the other cases, the respective moral orientations of the judge and the accused are shown to be different, and this has an important bearing on the relationship between judge and accused. Mbaezue cannot bring himself to believe that killing a man found with his wife constitutes an offence. In this, he is supported by tradition and the community. It is this delicate situation that the young inexperienced Officer, new from Scotland, with his fixed ideas of right and wrong, has to deal with. MacIntosh's attitude in this case of "attempted murder", looks forward to his uncompromising stand against the leaders of the community, when ritual murders are committed later. Why, one is entitled to ask, is MacIntosh, with his doctrinnaire attitude, given primary responsibility in these matters which might have been disposed of to the satisfaction of the villagers by the liberal and more experienced Mason? Throughout the novel, Mason is drawn in contrast to MacIntosh, both in his understanding of local customs and his anxiety to avoid direct confrontation with the villagers:

> I suggest that we shelve this matter, Mac. If the dead man's brother cares to come again and lodge a new complaint quite specifically — and doesn't change his story the next day when he's slept on it — then perhaps we'd be justified in having them in for questioning. But the way this matter stands now we just haven't a leg to stand on. Look, Mac, your man said one thing; then he changed his story; now with this letter he's gone back to his first one again. He's just not consistent, is he?[20]

This plea for caution and moderation by Mason is not heeded. MacIntosh pursues his perilous course and succeeds in alienating traditional authority from the Administration. It is clearly of the author's deliberate doing that any chance of reconciling the views and positions of both sides is irredeemably lost.

However much he tries, MacIntosh fails to establish a bridge of

---

[20] *ibid.*, pp. 75–6.

The Link Between Tradition and Modern Experience in the Nigerian Novel 59

understanding between his Administration and the people of Ukana. His fair decisions in court, his attempt to bring murderers to justice, his provision of amenities, his close attachment to his steward, are all turned against him and lead to an inevitable personal tragedy. With his repatriation, the Adminstration is discredited in much the same way as traditional authority has been. The author's treatment rules out compromise and accommodation and shows a severe reaction to the weaknesses of both sides.

V.

Okara avoids in *The Voice*, one of the main defects of *Many Thing You No Understand* — the tendency to point out the inadequacies of the past and present without suggesting a suitable alternative. Okara does much more than showing his feelings of disappointment with society. He probes deeply, the inner consciousness of his main character, converting his mind, in the process, into something of a battleground. Once his internal doubts are resolved, he rebels openly against a corrupt social order. The conflict in *The Voice*, is not so much one between the old and the new, as one between progressive and reactionary forces in contemporary society. It is a direct confrontation between Chief Izongo, the Elders and people on the one hand, and Okolo and the very few, who believe in him and his mission on the other. Okolo asks questions about the true meaning of life and, for this reason, is considered a threat to the established order. He is accused of behaving in a way tribal society cannot tolerate and made to pay the prescribed penalty. Okolo's problems, therefore, are those of a man, who finds himself unable to fit into the social framework of a society, in which the individual does not exist in his own right but is required to lose his identity in the interest of social cohesion. The novel comes down clearly, on the side of an individual code of conduct and the primacy of personal judgements, and shows an inherent distrust of a society which erects barriers against the free movement of the spirit.

Okara's method of attacking the corrupt-social and political order in Amata and Sologa, is to expose the people to ridicule as they consciously try to defend their moral decadence and morbid hatred of Okolo. By this method, he continually provides the reader an opportunity of analysing and evaluating character and conduct:

> "It was a great task I performed, my people. A great task in sending him away. A dangerous task, but it had to be done for the good of us all. We did it with our eyes on our occiputs, for it is a strong thing be to send away one who is looking for *it*. Only a mad man looks for *it* in this turned world. Let him look for *it* in this wide world if he can find *it*. But we don't want him to stay here asking, "Have you *it*? Have you *it*? Have you *it*?" Even in our sleep we hear him asking. We know not what *it* is. We do not want to know. Let us be as we are. We do not want our insides to be stirred like soup in a pot."[21]

Chief Izongo claims to have acted in the interest of his people by banishing Okolo. His hypocrisy is brought out in the use of words like "great" and "dangerous" and the distortion implicit in the highly technical language: "We did it with our eyes on our occiputs..." In fact, all Izongo has had to do is to order Okolo's banishment, which is carried out without hesitation by his henchmen. He partly justifies his action by asserting that "only a mad man looks for IT in this turned world." But the reader can only ragard this statement, judging by the way the story develops, as motivated by fear. In admitting that this is a "turned world", he might have gone further to acknowledge his own ignoble role in making it "turned". Okolo is a "mad man" only because he attempts to fight Izongo's moral and spiritual bankruptcy with the traditional weapons of honesty and integrity, values which Izongo, in his position, ought to be defending. There is a clear indication that, because of Izongo's resolute opposition to change — "Let us be as we are" — the conflict will be long-drawn and fierce. So, although this speech is enthusiastically received by gullible people, who sincerely believe that their Chief has done them a great service, the reader easily sees through Izongo's pretences and realizes that he has acted out of crude self-interest.

The rejection of Okolo, by the people, shows the extent to which they support Izongo in his nefarious purpose:

> Who is the leopard in town?
> Izongo!

---

[21] *The Voice*, p. 72.

Izongo!
And who is goat in town?
Oko-lo!
Oko-lo!
Can goat fight leopard?
No, no!
No, no![22]

The Elders and villagers, in a state of excitement at a drinks party, work themselves into a frenzy in their admiration of Izongo and their hatred of Okolo. Izongo is accorded the attributes of a leopard, a symbol of strength; Okolo, those of a goat which represents weakness. They rejoice that the leopard will slay the goat. But, because of the information we already have on these two characters, these symbols acquire an ironic meaning. Izongo's apparent strength lacks moral foundation and is put to corrupt use while Okolo's weakness stems from a genuine spirit of enquiry. So, a defeat of Okolo by Izongo can only be regarded as a temporary triumph of falsehood over truth.

The same type of irony informs Abadi's public rebuke of Okolo:

> "Why did you sulk in Tuere's house instead of coming to face the people? You should have still been in there hiding if not for the unparalleled gallantry of our leader who brought you running out like a rat. Listen not to him, fellow Elders. His mouth is foul. You and I are comrades in arms and we must see this thing through to its logical conclusion... We are in a democracy and everyone has the right to express any opinion."[23]

Abadi, Izongo's deputy, speaks of Amatu as a "democracy" where "everyone has the right to express any opinion." But the only reason Okolo is hounded from place to place is that he expresses an opinion unacceptable to the community. Tuere is ostracised because she too, expresses an opinion from which it is inferred that she is a witch. Abadi considers himself "in arms" against Okolo and promises to see "this thing through to its logical conclusion". But

---

[22] *ibid.*, p. 118.
[23] *ibid.*, p. 45.

he is later affected by Okolo's "spoken words" and virtually withdraws from Izongo's camp. An ironic contra-distinction between truth and falsehood is achieved by the use of expressions like "unparalleled gallantry" for Izongo and "His mouth is foul" for Okolo.

The Elders, as the acknowledged leaders of the people and the custodians of traditions and public morality, are the constant target of Okara's attack:

> Izongo : I am he-who-keeps-my-head-under-water!
> Second Elder : He-who-keeps-my-head-under-water!
> Izongo : Yes! His cloth will also touch water.!
> All Elders : Correct! Correct!
> Izongo : What is yours?
> Third Elder : Yes! He who touches me his fingers will burn! What is yours?
> Izongo : You are asking me? I am pepper.
> Third Elder : Pepper!
> Izongo : Yes; I am pepper. Pepper hurts but without it food is tasteless. And what is yours?
> Fourth Elder : I am bad waterside.
> Izongo : Bad waterside!
> Fourth Elder : I am! You will roll down if you are not careful.[24]

The Elders offer praise names ostensibly to illustrate the creative power of words in a traditional society. But none of these amounts to any distinct praise. Each name implies some disservice, either to the owner or the community. By making the Elders delight in platitudes — 'Pepper hurts but without it food is tasteless' — Okara gives the impression that they are a confused group, no longer certain of the values they claim to be defending.

It is through his preoccupation with his hero's "inside" that Okara gives the reader an insight into Okolo's disappointments and mental agony:

> Through the black black night Okolo walked, stumbled, walked. His inside was a room with chairs, cushions, papers scattered all over the floor by thieves. Okolo walked,

---

[24] *ibid.*, pp. 98–9.

stumbled, walked. His eyes shut and opened, shut and opened, expecting to see a light in each opening, but none he saw in the black black night.

As last the black black night like the back of a cooking pot entered his inside and grabbing his thoughts, threw them cut into the blacker than black night. And Okolo walked, stumbled, walked with an inside empty of thoughts except the black black night.[25]

This is the language of a lyrical poet who communicates almost exclusively through images and symbols. The "inside" of his here is, as it were, laid bare for the reader to see. It is turned into a living room invaded by thieves and the helplessness of the man is emphasized by deliberate repetitions — "walked, stumbled, walked", "shut and opened, shut and opened." His confusion is symbolized by the untidy state of the room and his disappointment, by his failure to replace darkness with light. The emphasis on darkness — "the black black night like the back of a cooking pot" — helps to make this evocation of desolation convincing.

Out of these doubts and disappointments emerge an inflexible resolve to continue the fight against Izongo and his henchmen. Given the circumstances of this confrontation, Okolo cannot be expected to win. But he makes spectacular gains. He enlists the active support of Tuere and Ukule and through the latter, Okolo is given the assurance: "Your spoken words will not die."[26] The second messenger vacillates in his support of Izongo; Ebiere, her husband and her brother throw aside traditional constraint and assert their youthful liberty. Even Abadi seems to accept Okolo at last. Furthermore, the hero's strategy for future action gives confidence

> This time he would the masses ask and not Izongo and his Elders. If the masses haven't got *it*, he will create *it* in their insides. He will plant *it,* make *it* grow in spite of Izongo's destroying words. He will uproot the fear in their insides, kill the fear in their insides and plant *it*. He will all these do.

---

[25] *ibid.,* p. 76.
[26] *ibid.,* p. 127.

Okolo has changed his tactics and decided on a new method of approach. Since he has failed with Izongo and the Elders, he will turn to the "masses" in his attempt to eradicate the materialistic value system with which the former have contaminated society. The struggle is not only political but ideological as well. The hero's determination to fight for the truth to the bitter end, is suggested by the repetition of his declared intention — "plant it", "make it grow"; "uproot the fear", "kill the fear" — and confirmed by "He will all these do".[27] Such a struggle between an established oligarchy and the masses, between truth and falsehood, has relevance for places and situations outside Amatu and Sologa. It is from such considerations that Okolo's activities derive their universal significance. Although not fully understood and accepted, Okolo's has been, to use Wole Soyinka's words, "the voice of vision in his own time"[28] and it ultimate victory is assured.

This vision is presented at both the human and symbolic levels. On the human level, what is stressed is that man everywhere can benefit from Okolo's experiences:

> Okolo sat with his knees drawn up to his chin trying not to touch anybody's body. This little he had now learned. He smiled in his inside. But is it possible for your body not to touch another body, for your inside not to touch another inside, for good or for bad?
> Is it possible to make your inside so small that nothing else can enter? Are spoken words blown away by the wind? No! Okolo in his inside saw. It is impossible not to touch another's inside. It is impossible to make your inside so small that nothing else can enter.... What of spoken words? Spoken words are living things like cocoa-beans packed with life.... So Okolo turned in his inside and saw that his spoken words will not die.[29]

Okolo gets into trouble on the way to Sologa when he is accused of "touching" Ebiere. On the return journey, he tries to avoid this type of situation by keeping to himself, far away from any other

---

[27] ibid., p. 90.
[28] Wole Soyinka, "The Writer in a Modern African State," *The Writer in Modern Africa*, ed. Per Wastberg (Uppsala, 1968), p. 21.
[29] *The Voice*, p. 110.

passenger — "This little he had now learned." The only way he can maintain this self-imposed separation is to sit "with his knees drawn up to his chin" — an inconvenient sitting position. Okara ridicules the idea of individual isolation, and we find ourselves agreeing with him — "Is it possible for your body not to touch another body, for your inside not to touch another inside, for good or for bad?" The Izongos of this world, who believe that all they have to do is to keep all the Okolos away to be secure in their wickedness and corruption deceive themselves. They are still exposed to the influence of "spoken words" which are "living things". It is the assurance that Okolo's spoken words "will not die", which makes the universal message of the novel an extremely hopeful one.

VI.

The attempt to create a link between tradition and modern experience poses many problems which, each of the authors dealt with in this article has tried to solve in his or her particular way. Some solutions, as we have seen, have proved more successful than others. Balewa's didactic use of folktales, his recreation of the glory and achievements of the past, especially the equanimity and stoic dignity which *Shaihu Umar* displays in the face of great odds, the convincing presentation of a society willing to be guided by high moral principles — all these are positive contributions from which the decoders of his message can benefit. This achievement has been possible partly because of the way in which the author, although relying on the resources of Hausa culture and language, has tried to avoid some of the problems of communication exhibited in Tutuola's works. Tutuola appears to have successfully solved many of his linguistic problems by depending almost entirely on Yoruba. But this, unfortunately, imposes some restrictions on his writings: by reducing the effect of any criticism of Yoruba society, past and present, it helps to create the impression that the novelist's attitude to indigenous culture is that of near uncritical total acceptance. It also sometimes obscures the intended link between tradition and modern life. This kind of solution holds very little promise for the future, since, it is based on a medium hardly capable of development. It would require the strange inventiveness of another Tutuola, for the English Language to be made to perform so successfully again the functions of the vernacular.

The way ahead to the future lies in the realistic manner in which novelists like Achebe, Aluko and Okara, intelligently adapt the English language to their artistic need. Achebe's works are extremely useful in the way they demonstrate some of the conditions which must be satisfied, if the Nigerian novelist concerned with indigenous culture is to communicate effectively: there is the need to employ themes which have a significant bearing upon real life and give a clear insight into the aspirations, hopes and fears of the age or society, the novelist is writing about. The background must either be fully realized as in *Things Fall Apart* and *Arrow of God* or convincingly consistent pictures of any changing or developing situations presented as in *No Longer at Ease* and *A Man of the People*.

Just as important as the material is the language. Achebe's successful example, results from the skilful way he renders Igbo language-process and speech patterns into English without rudely shocking the basic English sentence structure. Through a judicious use of the more symbolic elements of the Igbo language, such as proverbs and idioms, he makes it possible for his characters to speak in a manner any native speaker would recognize as natural to them. As was demonstrated earlier, Achebe's successful projection of the strengths and weaknesses of Igbo culture depends largely on his selection of episodes and skilful use of language.

An important theme, a consistent imaginative scheme, a language which recognizes the characteristics of L1 and skill in the use of language would, therefore, appear to be the essential requirements for the establishment of a successful link between tradition and modern experience. Only works which fulfil many of these conditions have a chance of achieving satisfactory results. Where an essential requirement is lacking, as in the novels of Miss Ulasi, the link is unsuccessful. No clear statements emerge from the works of Egbuna and Adaora Ulasi, because in each case the novelist displays a lack of creative intelligence. Transliteration of customs and traditions into modern terms, as attempted by them, provides the reader with little valuable experience. Although, like Okara, they subject indigenous culture to critical scrutiny, their works are too limited in intellectual and emotional range to form the basis of any assurance, in the circumstances of the twentieth century, that tradition will not be an obstacle to progress. However, they have been useful in the way they expose the type of artistic problems which must be solved in an attempt of this kind.

In *The Voice*, which grapples with these problems realistically, satisfactory results are achieved. The link between tradition and modern life is valuable only if it widens satisfyingly our experience of what it is to be human and thus, contributes to the solution of the political and social problems of the present, even if it does this in ways not at once materially obvious.

A significant feature of many Nigerian novels is the recognition of the tensions which exist between the impulse of the individual to experience life fully and live by a code of personal conduct, on the one hand, and the awareness, on the other hand, that one cannot, in spite of oneself, do without others, and, consequently, the assumptions and conventions which govern their lives. Achebe's works provide classic examples of this dilemma: If Okonkwo had had his way, he would have tried to circumvent the sanctions of society which prescribe banishment as the punishment for a female "ochu". However much he detests his stay at Mbanta, he finds that, once there, his best plan is to observe the customs of the people and rely for support and encouragement on his uncle, Uchendu, whose material help proves indispensable. Obi, too, would have preferred to sever all connections with the Umuofia Progressive Union and the people of Umuofia so that he could act freely, unhampered by any prejudice or traditional constraint. It is only without reference to the traditional elements in society that he can marry Clara. In spite of his drift towards modernity, such reference becomes necessary, and inevitably leads to disaster. In *Arrow of God*, Achebe achieves a delicate balance between the heavy responsibility which Ezeulu's position as Chief Priest of Ulu imposes on him and his personal desire to be associated early with Christianity. He acts with considerable foresight and sends his son, Oduche, to be his "eye" among the Christians. But his action is widely misinterpreted by the traditional forces in society, and is partly responsible for his eventual downfall. It would appear from these examples that in any confrontation between traditional and modern forces as the determiner of the fate of the chief character, traditional forces gain the upper hand.

The same conclusion will be substantially correct in respect of many other Nigerian novels. Although the customs, conventions and traditional practices of the people are usually criticized, the message seems to be that any individual who defies tradition does so at his own risk. Tradition is usually presented as a force, strong enough to make people comply with the social and cultural expectations of their society. So we find, for example, that, although the two main characters of *A Man of the People*, oppose each other violently, neither of them feels strong enough, even in their modern setting, to defy tradition. Balewa's characters are able to live down successfully, the cruelty of the days of slavery because of the inner strength provided them through their strict adherence to religious traditions. In Nzekwu's novels, the attempts made by Peter and Patrick to circumvent traditional requirements in the matters of marriage and religion respectively result in disaster in each case. In order to satisfy the judgements of society and against his personal inclination, Ekwueme in *The Concubine*, goes through the marriage ceremony with Ahurole even though, we are told, he does so as a "sleep-walker". Even Titus in *Kinsman and Foreman*, known for his respect for the truth and his great display of courage, fails to disclose in court and at the departmental Commission of Enquiry, all he knows about Simeon in deference to public, mostly traditional, opinion. It is only in *Danda* and *The Voice* that we have examples of Chief characters, who live by a code of personal conduct and get away with it, although not without a great deal of opposition from traditional and reactionary forces in society. The conflict between the past and the present, as these novels show, is the most important aspect of the attempt to create a link between tradition and modern experience. The unique achievement of successful Nigerian novelists like Achebe, Amadi, Okara and Aluko in this attempt has been made possible by their incisive analysis and evaluation of character and conduct, carried out with a subtlety and penetration which continually exercises and extends our understanding of human nature.

CHAPTER 5
T. M. ALUKO: THE NOVELIST AND HIS IMAGINATION*

I.

Aluko is the most undervalued Nigerian novelist. There is something amounting to a critical boycott of his novels. Standard works on the criticism of Nigerian Literature hardly make reference to him.[1] For example, none of his novels is considered good enough for treatment in Palmer's book on the African Novel.[2] Whenever references are made to Aluko's works they are usually brief and uncomplimentary. This tone of criticism was set by Ulli Beier in 1959 and has been followed with little change since then.[3] The only known geniune attempt to study Aluko as a novelist is that made in a recent short article by Bernth Linkfors.[4] The situation became so disturbing that Donatus Nwoga, in a recent comment on West African Literature, found it necessary to point out that "with the publication of *Chief the Honourable Minister....* T. M. Aluko has now an impressive record of four novels, a body of work which merits greater critical attention than it has yet received."[5]

II.

What has been responsible for the little critical notice which Aluko has received so far, and why has it been possible for him to be misunderstood for so long? Why do I so strongly believe

---

*First published in *Presence Africaine*, New Bilingual series, No. 90, 1974.
[1] See, for example, Bruce King ed., *Introduction to Nigerian Literature* (London, 1971).
[2] Eustace Palmer, *An Introduction to the African Novel* (London, 1972).
[3] See, for example, Ulli Beier in review of *One Man, One Wife*, *Black Orpheus*, 6 (1959), pp. 52–54; M. S. Dipoko in review of *One Man, One Wife*, *Presence Africaine*, 63 (1967), p. 263; S. O. Anozie in review of *Kinsman and Foreman*, *Presence Africaine*, 62 (1967), p. 203; *Margaret Laurence*, *Long Drums and Cannons* (London, 1968), p. 170; Vladimir Klima, *Modern Nigerian Novels* (Prague, 1969), p. 159.
[4] Bernth Lindfors. "T. M. Aluko: Nigerian Satirist," *African Literature Today*, No. 5 (1971), pp. 41–53.
[5] Donatus Nwoga in *The Journal of Commonwealth Literature*, Vol. 6, No. 2 (1971), 17.

that his works deserve more notice than they have got? For me, Aluko's importance lies in two significant areas of achievement: the first is his intimate knowledge of his people which has made it possible for him to establish a relevant link between tradition and modern experience; the second is his interest in the varieties of English as spoken and written in Nigeria.

Each of Aluko's works reveals how immensely, he has benefited as an artist from his incisive knowledge of the Yoruba as individuals and as a group. The four novels are based on a consistent imaginative scheme in which we have presented a society bound together by common beliefs and values but weakened by greed and intolerance.[6] The primary objective of the people is the pursuit of pleasure, and this is partly responsible for the types of characters we have in these novels. For, with the possible exception of Titus Oti in *Kinsman and Foreman,* none of them displays any degree of heroism. Their pre-occupation is to attain the necessary wealth, power and position which they almost invariably use for their own selfish ends. It is not surprising that in this type of situation there are frequent clashes of interest in matters political, social and economic. Occasionally, Aluko succeeds in fusing together in one single episode all these areas of conflict, as in the Igbodudu Land Dispute in *One Man, One Matchet.* But usually these interests are so diverse and irreconcilable that they are embodied in separate episodes.

Aluko's Western Nigeria is beset with fear and insecurity. To start with, there is the ever-present fear of one's enemies, visible and invisible. Any of these are considered capable of causing social or political harm to their opponents at any time. In a situation clouded by superstition and mistrust, it is not altogether surprising that people at times take ridiculous actions to safeguard their positions. An example of such an action is the oath-swearing ritual in the bedroom of the Prime Minister in *Chief the Honourable Minister*, in an attempt to settle a dispute between two Ministers of State, Alade Moses and Franco-John. Alade, who is dragged into the affair against his wish, gives us some idea of the weird ceremony:

---

[6] Page references are to the following African Writer's Series editions of the novels:
    One Man, One Wife (London, 1967).
    One Man, One Matchet (London, 1969).
    Kinsman and Foreman (London 1967).
    Chief the Honourable Minister (London, 1970).

Several weeks after, the whole thing still looked to him like a dream — the medico Prime Minister taking some blood with a syringe first from a vein in Franco-John's left forearm and then some from his own and emptying the contents into a white enamel dish already half filled with water. He saw dimly his relation Chief Odole saying some incantation, after which he first drank of the concoction himself. Perhaps that was to show that he was not poisoning the principal characters in the ceremony — if it was poison he was offering, then the poison would first affect him himself.[7]

Aluko's intention here is clearly satirical. First of all, there is the suggestion that the mutual distrust and suspicion between the two Ministers is so deep that it is not considered that peace can be restored between them without introducing a symbolic element of fear. It is the same kind of distrust which compels Chief Odole to drink of the "concoction" first. The word "concoction" not only points to the unpleasant nature of the drink but also suggests that, at best, it can only provide a make-shift remedy. There is also the irony of "the medico Prime Minister" who, many years after he had left medical practice for politics, now applies his medical skill in the wrong situation. This episode reveals the unhealthy psychological state of mind of the characters who are portrayed as the victims of fear.

Fear and discomfort are brought about not only by visible enemies. There is also an obsession with invisible evil forces which the people attempt all the time to ward off. For example, the whole atmosphere of *One Man, One Wife* is dominated by the fear of *Shonponna*, the god of smallpox. One reason why the Christian missionaries make little progress in Isolo is the people's fear of the dreadful consequences of abandoning their ancestral god, *Shonponna*, for the newfangled, incomprehensible idea which Christianity represents. As we are constantly reminded in these novels, a dead ancestor is not gone forever. He is only gone to heaven as a further extension of the extended family on earth and is capable of influencing his existing relations for good or bad. Even the conduct of government officials is influenced by the belief in the transmigration of souls as we see in *One Man, One Matchet*, when the Ministry of Agriculture's

---

[7] *Chief the Honourable Minister*, p. 105.

cutting-out squad avoid late Chief Ajayi's cocoa farm because of his assumed spiritual presence on the farm:

> The gang of tree-cutters cautiously avoided Chief Ajayi's farm. For Ajayi's ghost was known to haunt his house and his farm, and would continue to hover around his possessions here on earth, from which he was so violently separated, for a number of moons before finally betaking himself to a distant country where he was not known and where he would start another span of human existence under an entirely different name.[8]

The difference between fact and fiction is highlighted here by the juxtaposition of "ghost" and "human existence". The fact is that Ajayi is dead and gone forever; the fiction is that he "would continue to hover around his possessions... before finally betaking himself..." Although Aluko explains the concept of life after death from the point of view of those who believe in it, he makes the whole idea look ridiculous by putting his emphasis on the restlessness of Ajayi's ghost, and linking this with the tragi-comic manner of his death. The author's mocking tone comes out clearly in the use of expressions like "cautiously" (which points to the conscious effort of the tree-cutters), "was known to haunt" (which is far more circumstantial than is necessary), "betaking himself" and in the need for Ajayi to assume a "different name" in the "distant country".

An inevitable consequence of these superstitious beliefs is the creation of a situation in which rumour and gossip thrive. These play unusually important parts in Aluko's works and are employed for the most part to make the confused world of these novels more confounded. Occasionally, however, they provide humour and are used for the relief of tension. In *One Man, One Wife*, when Jacob disappears for a few days after his court case with Toro, varied and fantastic accounts are offered for his temporary disappearance, the most colourful being that he has been taken away on the wings of Archangel Gabriel. In the same manner, in *One Man, One Matchet*, many far-fetched explanations are given at Ipaja of Benjamin Benjamin's accident and stay in hospital at Apeno, including the preposterous suggestion that he has been jailed by Udo Akpan. These unfounded rumours, which are allowed to influence the

---

[8] *One Man, One Matchet*, p. 108.

course of events to an incredible extent, prove that in the Yoruba society of Aluko's fictional creation, most of the people are credulous and uncritical, and thus, fair game for satire.
Practically every aspect of the life of the people is heavily criticized by the novelist. An important feature of this society is its conservative attitude — a predisposition to reject anything new or capable of upsetting old ways of life. This characteristic it shares to some extent with Achebe's Igbo society. It rejects a new religion in *One Man, One Wife*, a truly beneficial economic proposition in *One Man, One Matchet* and an atte.npt to introduce a new dimension into family relationships in *Kinsman and Foreman*. But to the credit of the same society it stands resolutely against, and triumphs over, a system of social and economic exploitation in *Chief, the Honourable Minster*. Dramatic tension is provided in this novel by the unrelenting opposition of the majority of the people to the political abuses and electoral fraud practised by the Ministers and party functionaries of the Freedom for All Party. In this respect, they display a greater political consciousness than the society of Achebe's *A Man of the People*, which remains largely indifferent to the corrupt activities of politicians.

Religion, especially Christianity, in which these novels show a great deal of interest, is presented with a measure of satire. In each of the first three novels, a priest plays a prominent role in the development of the action. For example, in *One Man, One Wife*, the Christian Mission, Rev. David and his assistant, Teacher Royasin, provide most of the action of the novel. As might be expected, initially they have a very difficult time; in fact, at no time during their ministration can they claim complete success. Their difficulties and modest achievements are symbolically represented by the peculiar behaviour of a kerosene lamp at the Mission House at Isolo:

> Pastor and Teacher watched the flickering flame. It appeared to be fighting a gasping battle against unseen forces wanting to choke it out of existence. The gasps were spasmodic, the flame looked like going out after every one. Then it seemed to recover and flicker into life again for a brief period.... The flame slowly regained steadiness and confidence. Its light rose steadily in intensity...[9]

The sustained metaphor here gives a vivid impression of the situation.

---

[9] *One Man, One Wife*, p. 13.

The operative word is "gasping", which successfully describes the initial difficulties Christian missionaries had in making any impression on the people of Isolo against the "unseen forces" of ignorance and superstition. At first, it looked as if the "flame" must be choked out of existence by the stronger forces of tradition. But because of the energetic evangelical work of Rev. David, the "flickering flame" regains "steadiness and confidence". Aluko succeeds in this short paragraph in setting the pattern which is followed in his first three novels in the encounter between Christianity and traditional religion.

It is appropriate that religion plays very little part in *Chief, the Honourable Minister*. As in *A Man of the People*, the progressive moral degeneration of the leaders of the people has proceeded so far and they have become so unconscionable and ruthless in their political behaviour that they are not likely to benefit from the admonitions of a priest. Aluko shows intimate knowledge of the society he writes about. That is why, for example, he imaginatively accepts the duality of the life of the typical Yoruba, the type of situation which makes it possible for him, for instance, to worship with a church congregation in the morning and offer sacrifices to his ancestors in the evening without suffering from any mental conflict. This is the way Simeon behaves in *Kinsman and Foreman*. "The deistic approach of the Yoruba," says Wole Soyinka, "is to absorb every new experience, departmentalize it and carry on with life."[10] The desire to carry on with life, preferably in conditions of ease and quiet, provides the necessary motivation for Aluko's characters and is manifest even in the actions, songs, prayers and proverbs of the society he presents. An example is provided by this short modern Yoruba pop song:

> Ma a ko'le
> Ma a bi'mo
> Ma ramoto ayokele
> Laisi alafia
> Wonyen ko se ise
> Alafia loju
> Ilera loro
> Eniti o ni alafia
> O lohun gbogbo

---

[10] Wole Soyinka, "From a Common Black Cloth: A Reassessment of the African Literary Image," *AMSAC Newsletter*, Vol. 6, No. 6 (1964), pp. 4–5.

I want to build a house,
I want to have children,
I want to have a motor-car.
Without peace,
These things are impossible,
Peace is supreme,
Health is wealth,
He who has peace,
Has everything.[11]

This song points to material values and an attitude of mind which Aluko does not share. He uses these, usually in an ironic sense, to carry forward the purpose of satire.

Aluko's presentation of Yoruba society shows how preoccupied he is with the present, especially the conflicts and abuses which appear in daily life. His themes are based on the conventional subjects of poverty, ignorance, disease, religion and struggle for power, which he often treats with real insight. His method is to stay close to social reality in the treatment of events. For, as Eldred Jones has pointed out;

> The writer today in Africa must see around him bad politics, bad religion, the misleading of ordinary people, and he is bound to write about all this if he writes about his environment. Of course, he can decide to opt out of it altogether, to write space fiction or something like that. But I feel that the writer has to write about what happens around him...[12]

This is what Aluko does. When he looked around him in Western Nigeria in the fifties, he saw, among other evils, a large measure of "bad politics" and "the misleading of ordinary people". It is this experience that he has communicated artistically successfully to his readers.

---

[11] Dele Ojo: "Alafia," Philips West African Records No. PFB 898 quoted in J. Awolalu. "The Yoruba Philosophy of Life", *Presence Africaine*. No. 73 (1970), pp. 21–22.

[12] Eldred Jones in his contribution to Wole Soyinka, "The Writer in a Modern African State," *The Writer in Modern Africa* (Uppsala, 1968), pp. 34–35.

III.

His second area of achievement is closely connected with his method of presentation. Aluko presents his material in a way which shows clearly his keen observation of the various ways English is used by both literate and illiterate people in Nigeria. The problems of communication which arise from these works reflect this concern. What seems to be of particular interest to the novelist is the inappropriateness of the use of language in various situations and for various purposes. That is why, we find in these novels a greater variety of English registers, as commonly used in Nigeria, than in those of many other Nigerian novelists. There is, for example, the language of people like Jacob, a semi-literate who can barely use the English Language correctly; then there are characters like Benjamin Benjamin and Royasin who, although literate, use language as a means of deceiving gullible villagers. Aluko also uses, as appropriate, the language of journalism and the Civil Service to show the sorts of things which can go wrong with language in the hands of demogogues and overzealous civil servants. It is this kind of interest which Aluko shows in the use of language and the problems of communication generally, which accounts for the large number of cliches, "journalese" and "officialese" in his works. As will soon become evident, these are employed deliberately for satiric ends.

In *One Man, One Wife*, for example, a great deal centres on Royasin's dishonest use of language. In his opposition to the Church in his new capacity as "Public Letter-writer and Notary, Friend of the Illiterate, Advocate of the Oppressed", Royasin wins enough popular support to be able to embarrass the Christians. His position soon becomes so unassailable that many sections of the community look up to him for help and advice. This is part of a letter he writes to *The Nigerian Recorder* on behalf of the people of Isolo:

> All the inhabitants of this ancient village – men, women, boys and girls and children – they all opened wide their mouths in wonder and astonishment and curiosity when they discovered and disclosed the identity of the manager of the thieves and robbers; for he was one important and importable member of the the Church at Isolo. The law of libel and slander and scandal forbids and forbodes a newspaper cor-

respondent from correspondingly disclosing the name of this leader of the culprits.[13]

Aluko uses newspaper articles in his novels for satirical effect. Royasin's use of *The Nigerian Recorder*, is a good example of how a mass communication medium can be thoroughly abused. As soon as he falls out with his boss and is dismissed from his post, he turns against the Church and uses the newspaper as a platform of a bitter attack and full-scale revenge on the Church, calling its leaders rogues and vagabonds. His language is that of a semi-literate writer, who wants to impress others with his prodigious knowledge of the English language. Many of the linguistic characteristics of Yoruba-repetition, exaggeration and word-play — are featured here, and are blatantly used for effect — "wonder" and "astonishment", "discovered", and "disclosed", "thieves" and "robbers", not to mention the comically unintended malapropism "importable" for "important" and "forbodes" for "forbids". The writer is so anxious for revenge and so full of hatred for Pastor David that he communicates only with difficulty. As Aluko says, "as for Pastor David, the ex-Catechist would go to the ends of the earth to put that man in real trouble."[14] Royasin's journalistic activities broaden the area of conflict between him and the Christians and incite Pastor David to further evangelical work. The more successful Rev. David is in his mission, the more embittered and vociferous Royasin becomes.

Even in cases where Royasin intends to be of help to his friends his approach is usually a very clumsy one:

> I beg your Honour most respectfully and respectively to carefully and patiently peruse these few lines of a tale of woe and persecution and prosecution perpetrated and perpetuated on your Honour's most unworthy servant, to wit my humble self, Longe of Idoka Village...
>
> The land that is the subject of this abominable act of man's inhumanity to man is the land of your Honour's respectful, respective, unworthy servant, to wit my humble self Longe, of Idoka Village... The land was the undisputed and absolute property of the renowned forebears of your Honour's most

---

[13] *One Man, One Wife*, p. 125.
[14] *Ibid.*, p. 127.

humble and unworthy servant. In the unwritten but verbal, verbose and oral history of Adasaland, the large piece of land was very generously and royally given by His Highness Oba Atakumasa, to his humble subject and loyal general for valiantly and courageously driving out the soldiers of the King of Ibadan away from Adasa Territory.[15]

This is part of the petition which Royasin writes in his characteristic bombastic English to the District Officer, Idasa, on behalf of Longe who has allegedly been deprived of his land. It is by stroke of luck that a long pedantic petition like this succeeds. Through such parody Aluko deliberately presents the reader with the problem of separating fact from fiction and of sorting out the significant from the trivial, the original from the merely repetitive — "respectfully and respectively", "carefully and patiently", "persecution and prosecution", "perpetrated and perpetuated", "unwritten and verbal", "valiantly and courageously". The pervasive use of cliches and stereotyped expressions — "your Honour's most unworthy servant", "this abominable act of man's inhumanity to man", "his humble subject and loyal general", "to wit my humble self, Longe" — underlines Royasin's total lack of originality. Although he occasionally achieves good results, as in this case, the impression of Royasin that a letter like this creates is of a man, who is full of his own importance and is determined to impose himself at all costs on his illiterate community.

The exaggerations and repetitions in Aluko serve careful satirical purposes and show his technical sophistication in the matter of handling language. It is when considered against such a background that this Christmas message, for example, coming as it does from Royasin (even though given in reported speech) acquires an ironic significance:

> CHRISTMAS!
> It comes but once a year. The little knot of Christians of Isolo listened devotedly to Royasin propound in the village church its story, its message and its lesson. The story of the birth of the Boy Jesus born to the Virgin Mary and how He subsequently founded the greatest and only true religion in

---

[15] *Ibid.*, p. 85.

the world. The message of peace on earth and goodwill to all men in all lands and where at all hours of that sacred day various voices were being lifted up in prayer and in praise to the Boy born to be King. The lesson of humility — that to serve and save mankind the Lord Jesus had to descend to human level and assume human form, and had to be born not to the king's queen on her throne, but to a carpenter's wife in the horses' stables.[16]

The Christians may listen "devotedly", but they have nothing to gain from Royasin's examples. Here, we have the case of a man, who is himself far from humble preaching "the lesson of humility". Aluko reports the sermon in a way which reflects the speaker's hackneyed phrasing and his revelling in the grandiose glory of his subject. The village church is hardly the right place to "propound" any theories about Christmas. In any case, there is nothing inspiring in the way the message is presented to the audience — what we have is a tedious restatement of pious platitudes — "it comes but once a year". It ought to have occurred to the speaker that very few people in the audience are likely to be hearing of the Christmas message for the first time.

The reader cannot help feeling that Royasin becomes important only because of the social context in which he finds himself, one which he fully exploits to his own advantage. If he is accepted by the villagers as a saviour, it is only because his unscrupulous methods occasionally succeed and because the people are too ignorant and indifferent to discover his faults. So when, for example, a drummer in a state of excitement sings Royasin's praises:

> Royasin, Royasin,
> Son of Royasin, Chief Osi Oba of Idasa.
> Royasin, Royasin,
> The wizard who knows the White Man's secrets.
> The wizard who reads telegrams and writes letters.
> The wizard who understands and speaks the White Man's strange tongue.
> Royasin, Royasin,
> Son of Royasin, Chief Osi Oba of Idasa.[17]

---

[16] *Ibid.*, p. 66.
[17] *Ibid.*, p. 71.

The reader realizes the drummer is acting in ignorance. To the drummer Royasin may be a "wizard" because he can read and write and speak "the White Man's strange tongue". To the reader, he is an unscrupulous man, who devotes his energy and skill to the deceit and exploitation of his people. He is a memorable character only because of the part he plays in helping to make the world of this novel a confused one. In his opposition to the Church, he succeeds in generating so much tension that the Christians end up just as confused as the adherents of traditional religion.

Like Royasin, other characters in the novel are satirized through the kind of language the author puts in their mouths or bestows on their pens. For example, Aluko gives us an insight into the character of Jacob through the letter he writes to his father, Joshua, the beginning of which reads:

> To my dear Father,
> Mr. Joshua,
> Isolo Village,
> Idasa District.
>
> With much gladness of heart and love I write to you this letter. I hope that it will get to you in peace and in good health as I am here. I am very well, and there is nothing to complain about. For this and other blessings Jehovah's name be praised.
>
> I received the letter which you wrote to me. My dear father, my joy was exceedingly great when I saw the letter. I opened the envelope and I read the letter. All the matters that you wrote about I understood. I thank you greatly for this, Father. You are a good father to me.[18]

We have no difficulty in establishing from this letter that Jacob is a semi-literate person. Through his literal translation from the Yoruba in which the letter was originally written, the novelist both confirms the low degree of literacy of the writer and suggests his social status. The first two sentences in the original would have read:

---

[18] *Ibid.*, p. 28.

Pelu inu didun ati ife ni mo fi kowe yi si yin. Mo si rope yio
ba yin ni ayo ati alafia bi mo ti wa nihin.[19]

This is not only a word-for-word translation but it takes a familiar
pattern which has almost become a formula for semi-literate people
writing Yoruba. There are other pointers to aspects of Jacob's
character in this letter — his casual reference to Jehovah, the needless
recapitulation of the steps he took when the letter arrived — he "saw
the letter", "opened the envelope" and "read the letter". His
enthusiastic praise of his father as being "good" is not borne out
by the rest of the letter in which he accuses his father of forcing
Toro on him. The overall impression created of Jacob from this
letter is that of a man who is excited because he can do any writing
at all, naive in his beliefs and given to facile assumption.

IV.

Benjamin Benjamin's use of language as a means of deceiving the
people is the centre of interest in *One Man, One Matchet*. In his
handling of *National Affairs*, the author shows how completely
unscrupulous Benjamin Benjamin can be. *National Affairs* is used
as a rallying point of opposition to the economic plans of the
Government. In the hands of a demagogue like Benjamin Benjamin,
the attempt completely succeeds. One is reminded of the Nigerian
nationalists' reliance on the local press during the struggle for independence. The tactics are the same — you deny your opponents
any kind of merit and, for effect, exaggerate the wrong that has
been done to your people, who but for the imposition of a Colonial
Government would have been living a life of bliss. In a typical
article in *National Affairs*, Benjamin Benjamin complains of excessive
tax assessments:

> The Ipajas as a people are known to be law-abiding. Even
> before they conquered the Apenos and ruled the whole
> country before the White Man came, they were essentially
> men of peace. But owing to the excesses of their neighbours
> they were forced to draw the sword, and to show them their
> supremacy in the science of war and military tactics.

---

[19] This translation, which is a literal one, is mine.

> Today the temper of the descendants of the brave Ipajas of old is being tried. This time the agressors are not their traditional enemies the Apenos. At least not on the surface. The agressors are the Administrative Officers who are asking the poor farmers to pay exorbitant taxes. Old men and women are being taxed most harshly. Tax assessments bear no relation to the proved means of income of the people. Fantastic and preposterous. Absolutely ridiculous, the taxes that infirm men and children are being called upon to pay in Ipaja.[20]

Benjamin Benjamin plays on the idea of the antiquity and military prowess of the "brave" and "law-abiding" Ipajas — "man of peace", who were harassed in ancient times by their neighbours and now by new "aggressors". The charge that Government officials, who are expected to be impartial in inter-village disputes like the Igbodudu Land Case, are supporting the Apenos against the Ipajas, if proved, could ruin the career prospects of such officials. Benjamin Benjamin knows that the charge is not true but makes it nonetheless, in order to embarrass Udo Akpan, his mortal enemy. He uses highly emotive words like, "exorbitant" (in relation to the level of tax the people are asked to pay) and "fantastic and preposterous", to describe the whole situation — all in an attempt to bring home to the people the enormity of the crime being perpetrated against them. The reference to "old men and women" is the sort of sentiment, he knows is capable of winning him support in a society which places such a high premium on age. On the other hand, the suggestion that "infirm men and children" are called upon to pay tax is merely ridiculous. These misrepresentations and exaggerations achieve their purpose of finally inciting the villagers to riot and murder but leave the reader in no doubt of Benjamin Benjamin's ruthlessness and dishonesty.

Like Royasin in *One Man, One Wife*, Benjamin Benjamin is a semi-literate man who is extremely anxious to be regarded by the illiterate villagers as a man of great learning:

> The White Man has a proverb. A beautiful proverb. You know what it is?

---

[20] *One Man, One Matchet*, pp. 82 83.

No, they did not. They wanted the great Benjamin
Benjamin to tell them.
Yes, I will tell you the proverb. "No one puts his hand on
the plough and looks back." Again there is another proverb.
"We have crossed the Rubicon." There is no going back.[21]

Here is Benjamin Benjamin performing at a village assembly which he turns into a lecture theatre. He insists on telling the people a White Man's "beautiful" proverb, but ends up offering two; one of these is trivial and distorted, the other almost completely irrelevant to the situation. Benjamin Benjamin is "great" not in any laudable sense, but in his pompous and shameless attempt to impose himself on others.

The novelist puts Benjamin Benjamin in several situations which expose his personal weaknesses and insincerity:

"Fathers, Mothers, Elders, Youths. Fellow patriots of Ipaja —
my comrades-in-arms. I salute you all for your great victory
in this great battle of right against might. The victory is yours.
I am no more than the unworthy medium through whom the
founder of Ipaja has brought it to you." He stopped. His
words did not fail to bring the applause he intended. He
continued: "When I see you like this, solidly behind me,
demonstrating in no uncertain terms your stand for freedom
and right and your demand for the restoration of the land,
the fertile land that your fathers owned before you but which
was stolen by the White Man and given to your enemy the
Apenos — I weep for joy."
He wept. He brought out a silk handkerchief and wiped
the tears from his eyes. It produced the desired effect.[22]

This display of emotion before his people may produce "the desired effect", but it only helps to confirm our impression of his unscrupulousness. The operative phrase is "unworthy medium". Benjamin Benjamin uses this expression as an intentional understatement in an attempt to project a false image of himself as a humble servant of the people. But, ironically, from the reader's point of view, this

---

[21] *Ibid.*, p. 81.
[22] *Ibid.*, pp. 138–39.

is the most appropriate description of him, judged by his activities and their effects on the people. Even the "great victory" he is celebrating here is wholly undeserved — he has been acquitted of charges of embezzlement of public funds not because he is innocent but because, as the megistrate makes clear, he has been charged under the wrong section of the law. Although Benjamin Benjamin calls the people of Ipaja "my comrades-in-arms", it is these people whose ignorance he has been exploiting all the time to further his own selfish ends. He makes much of the fact that he understands the White Man's language and soon establishes himself as an intermediary between the people and the Administration. In this capacity he abuses the Apaja's confidence in him, robs Olowokere of £50 and lines his pocket from the three different Funds he gets going at the same time. This type of behaviour gives "comrades-in-arms", an ironic significance in much the same way as "the victory is yours", comes to acquire an ironic meaning in the context of the novel as a whole. Benjamin Benjamin uses the latter expression in the spirit of fraternal rejoicing, in a show of identifying himself closely with his people. But, ironically, the one great victory won by the Ipajas in the novel is the way they succeed in getting rid of Benjamin Benjamin where the British system of justice has failed. It is by continually bringing before the reader the difference between what Benjamin Benjamin says and what he does, the difference between what he pretends to be and what he actually is, that Aluko satirizes this character. Although, he is regarded by the people at the height of his career as a national hero, the reader recognizes him all the time as an "unworthy medium", a man with an unlimited capacity for doing evil. That is why, we find ourselves able to agree with this damaging description of him given by the magistrate:

> I find him to be a perfect example of the man with the proverbial half learning which is a dangerous thing. He is self-opinionated, with an extremely exaggerated idea of his own importance, and his mendacity is extraordinary. It is my considered opinion that he is a grave danger to the community in which he lives, a tragedy to the cause of education in this country, and a curse on humanity as a whole.[23]

---

[23]*Ibid.*, p. 133.

That almost certainly is the point of view shared by the novelist. It is also through his own-use of language that Benjamin Benjamin's antagonist, Akpan, is satirized. The new African District Officer talks of tackling problems in an essentially African way but behaves like any expatriate District Officer, a situation which earns him the appellation of "the black White Man". He is an idealist, who cannot bring himself to believe that any rational basis exists for the people's opposition to the Government's economic proposals and for their longing for modern amenities while they refuse to pay tax. However, he is not portrayed, like Benjamin Benjamin, as a man without redeeming features. He shows great efficiency in his administrative work. For example, he conducts the Commission of Enquiry into the fund-raising activities of Benjamin Benjamin with remarkable speed and thoroughness and in his report uses language appropriate to his social status and office, though here we recognize the satirical note again:

> Mr. Benjamin Benjamin, the Secretary-General of the Ipaja Descendants' Union, also failed to come to give evidence at the Inquiry. He no doubt was acting in accordance with the advice of the lawyer. My confidential inquiry at the office of the Attorney General as to my powers in these circumstances has not been answered yet. No doubt the experts are still looking into the legal aspects. Needless to say how disappointing and sad it is that the person who should have been key witness in the Inquiry has absented himself from the Inquiry and at the time of writing we do not see our way clear towards taking any active measure against him. I refrain from saying anything further at this stage about Mr. Benjamin Benjamin, realizing as I do that a man must be presumed innocent until proved guilty.[24]

This is the language of the Civil Service, the style of a man aiming to be "correct" in all he does. He writes to the office of the Attorney-General about the extent of his powers and refrains from making unofficial remarks about Benjamin Benjamin, a man who makes his work at the Enquiry infinitely more difficult. His "correct" attitude is shown by his acceptance of the fact that "a man must

---

[24] *Ibid.*, p. 131.

be presumed innocent until proved guilty", an admirable principle in itself, no doubt, yet partaking in its expression of the same cliched "officialese" as phrases like "key witness" and "active measure". Akpan's addiction to the "correct" is associated with his odd conviction that all that is needed for the people to accept the colonial situation is to make the system work efficiently — the people's deep-seated opposition to the system is of little importance to him. This is one reason why he devotes so much energy to the Commission of Enquiry and shows so much resentment against the law officers when, Benjamin Benjamin is allowed to escape punishment for his offences on technical grounds. Again, characteristically, he blames the confused situation which follows the murder of Benjamin Benjamin on Pax Britannica:

> Before you came to this country with Pax Britannica, a citizen of proved anti-community activities like Benjamin Benjamin was easily disposed of. He just vanished.... After we in the Administration had failed to rid ourselves of the curse that was Benjamin Benjamin, an Ipaja man who had not heard of British sense of fair play and justice and in any case had no use for it got rid of the common enemy. He did it in a moment. We had failed to do it in two years.[25]

Not only Akpan but also the Colonial Administration are satirized here. Akpan is over-reacting to the situation created by Benjamin Benjamin's death. We are presented with the ironical situation in which a "modern" Administrative Officer advocates the revival of the old method of punishing criminals. Yet if the African idea of summary justice were to be applied in all cases, it would affect not only Akpan's enemy, Benjamin Benjamin, but also his friend, Rev. Olaiya, who constantly violates customary laws. "He just vanished," indeed, recalls what happens to Rev. Olaiya when he is taken away by members of a secret cult and becomes a wanted man for forty-three days. "He did it in *a moment*", applied in contradistinction to "We had failed to do it in *two years*", epitomizes the essentially simple-minded ideal of ruthless efficiency which Akpan desires for the Civil Service. He resigns his appointment when he realizes that, "there is just no future for the African in

---

[25] *Ibid.*, p. 187–88.

the present set-up of the administration of his own country."²⁶ In him we have the portrait of a young African District Officer, who finds himself in an invidious position — he is alienated from his fellow Africans because of his single-minded devotion to duty in the Colonial Service but finally has to leave the Service because "there is no self-respecting African who would want to identify himself with the present set-up."²⁷

V.

In *Chief the Honourable Minister*, Aluko dramatizes a situation in which language is used dishonestly by both Government and Opposition politicians to achieve undesirable political objectives. "The misleading of ordinary people" is practised on a wide scale, and the Prime Minister, himself, sets a bad example in a passage like this, full of far-fetched comparisons and allusions:

> A great English scholar once observed that when we see genius come out of what looks like the gutter we should know that it did not begin there. If we take the trouble to dig beneath the surface we will discover that like Shakespeare the son of a wood-pedlar, Napoleon the son of a farmer, and Luther the son of a peasant, the genius from the gutter most probably descended from a line of kings and prophets. That observation was made about one of the greatest figures of history, Abraham Lincoln. It may well be applied here and now to your own son Alade Moses.²⁸

The aim of the Prime Minister is to improve the image of Alade Moses by comparing him with some great names in history. The reader quickly appreciates the inappropriateness of these comparisons. Not only has Moses little in common, to put it mildly, with these heroes of the past; the comparison in nearly every case is made in a sloppy manner. But then the Prime Minister is addressing a crowd of illiterate and semi-literate people, who are not in a position to discover the flaws in his comparisons. It is only in such

---
²⁶ *Ibid.*, p. 166.
²⁷ *Ibid.*
²⁸ *Chief the Honourable Minister*, p. 176.

circumstances that a speech like this succeeds in its purpose. It is mainly through the use of such ironies, usually arising from the conflict of ideas and personalities, that Aluko achieves in this work the purpose of satire which is his chosen method of establishing a link between tradition and modern experience.

The type of political instability presented in this work, the intrigues and rivalries vividly and sharply described and the many examples of clashes of personalities and ideas between Government and Opposition politicians take the reader very close to the pattern of politics in Nigeria which led to the Civil War. There are many instances of political jobbery, officially planned and carefully executed. One such example is the decision of the Executive Council that Government contracts should be awarded only to party supporters. This creates a problem for Alade Moses who does not know how to inform his Permanent Secretary and his Director of Public Works, both British, of the new decision which he himself considers outrageous and indefensible:

> He hardly knew how to begin it. Just how did one say to a civil servant that contracts for government works financed from public funds should not be given out to the men who by knowledge, experience, and financial standing were most suitable for them but that they should be given to the shoemakers, the barbers, and the unattached women with painted lips, the new class of society known as Party supporters?[29]

Moses states in this passage what criteria he would have liked to insist upon for the award of contracts — "knowledge, experience and financial standing". The reasonableness of his position is brought out clearly by the implied comparison with the sort of people to whom, for political reasons, Government building contracts will now go — "the shoemakers, the barbers and the unattached women with painted lips" — people, who know nothing about the construction industry. The whole idea is made to look ridiculous. The inclusion of "unattached women with painted lips", sarcastically points to an important area of weakness among these politicians. Political malpractices, indeed, are so widespread that wherever, the novelist turns his attention, he discovers crude political behaviour

---

[29] *Ibid.*, p. 143.

and an inordinate attempt to ride on the backs of others to political success.
There is little to choose between the Government and the Opposition. The Government is corrupt and the Opposition employs unscrupulous methods to destroy it. The *Sentinel* is made the voice of the Opposition and the means of exposing the corrupt practices of Government. As the Government becomes more unpopular with the people, the *Sentinel* increases in circulation and becomes a more effective means of articulating the wishes of the people. Aluko appears particularly sensitive to the powers of the Press in the formulation and direction of public opinion. In its attempt to reflect the feelings of the people, the attitude of the *Sentinel* to the Government of the Freedom for All Party is one of antagonism and bitter hatred:

> The wrath of the God of Africa will descend upon them, the perpetrators of this monstrous crime against the electorate of the nation. And Nemesis will come to all the organs and institutions of society that have aided and abetted the crime. All of them that have made a complete mockery of the sacred institution of the ballot box, all of them that stood in the way of the people's exercising their inalienable right to choose who shall speak for them in the nation's assembly — all of them will pay the penalty at the appointed time.[30]

Although the objective of members of the Opposition appears to be a laudable one — the overthrow of a corrupt and unpopular Government — they do not inspire confidence that, in Government, they will do better than those they now seek to replace. They employ the same demagogic methods to whip up national emotion as those for which Benjamin Benjamin becomes famous in *One Man, One Matchet*. The exaggerations and unnecessary repetitions in the passage — "perpetrators of this monstrous crime", "organs and institutions of society", "aided and abetted", "complete mockery" — the pervasive use of cliches — "sacred institution", "inalienable right" — adversely affect the way we respond to the situation. "God of Africa" is a rhetorical ploy calculated to play on the passions and prejudices of the masses. And even though "Nemesis" looks

---

[30] *Ibid.*, p. 32.

forward to the coup at the end of the novel when all politicians, whether in Government or Opposition, "pay the penalty at the appointed time" for their greed and selfishness, the *Sentinel* uses the word only for its vague impressiveness.

As Leader of the Opposition, Dauda, in particular, uses the *Sentinel* in the most sensational way to embarrass the Government and create tension. When, for example, as a result of a petition organized by him, Moses' election to Parliament is nullified by the High Court, he takes advantage of the occasion to come down heavily on the Government. The language of this article is typical of Dauda:

> We of this paper have been justified in our unshaken belief in the unlimited capacity of our judiciary to absorb the stresses and strains to which this unholy gang of rascals who have now forced themselves upon the nation have subjected the judges and the magistrates. In the dark days of every nation when rogues and dictators seize the reins of government it has always been the impartiality, fearlessness, and incorruptibility of the custodians of justice that have always stood between man and doom. We are proud to record here to the eternal glory of the judiciary of this land that in spite of threats and intimidation, most times subtle and concealed but sometimes open, they have carried out their sacred duty of administering justice, just justice, in the highest tradition of their most sacred calling.[31]

Members of the Cabinet are called "this unholy gang of rascals", "rogues and dictators" — all in an attempt to bring the Government into disrepute. The impression given of Dauda is that of a man anxious to achieve his goal by any means, fair or foul. The reason the Bench is brought in for high praise is their recent verdict, favourable to him. But this praise is communicated in such stilted language that the reader takes it no more seriously than the blame directed elsewhere — "In the dark days of every nation... it has always been the impartiality, fearlessness, and incorruptibility of the custodians of justice that have always stood between man and doom." Other hackneyed expressions like "to the eternal glory of the judiciary",

---

[31] *Ibid.*, pp. 154–55.

"their sacred duty", "just justice", "in the highest tradition of their most sacred calling", similarly point to Dauda's hollowness.

But for Alade Moses, on whose psychological development the novelist devotes much attention, there would have been a complete gulf between the two sets of politicians. His activities provide the only link, although usually an unhappy one, between the Government in which he is Minister of Works and the Opposition, who take a special interest in his activities. He is usually the target of Dauda's vicious attacks. These attacks are not entirely without justification. For Moses drifts gradually, almost unwittingly, from a position of moral strength at the beginning of the novel, to a deplorable situation at the end, when he becomes almost as ruthless as his colleagues in the Cabinet. In this aspect of his development, he reminds one of Odili. But the changes which overtake Moses come more gradually and imperceptibly. It is only towards the end of the novel that the reader begins to notice the effect of these changes, but they have been taking place all the time. The changes in Moses reveal themselves more in the doubts and mental agony he exhibits than in overt actions.

Given this situation, the Prime Minister's eulogy of Moses at a public meeting where the latter is installed Asiwaju of Newtown is important, in an ironic sense, in the context of the novel as a whole:

> We are all here today not just because he belongs to our great Party but because he is a great man with whom we are proud to associate... Above all we are glad that you have by conferring this chieftaincy on your greatest son helped him, you have helped us, you have helped this nation, to rediscover this great man, this prophet that has been going in and coming out among you in this progressive town without your recognizing his worth, his noble ancestry....[32]

Such high praise might just conceivably have been appropriate for Moses at the beginning of his political career. Considering the fact that he has now failed to live up to his lofty ideals, the reader can no longer regard him as, "a *great* man with whom we are proud to associate." The repeated promiscuous emphasis placed on the word "great" reveals Aluko's sardonic intent. The people of Newtown

---

[32] *Ibid.*, p. 176.

are said to have "helped" Moses, their town and country by "recognizing" Moses' worth. But, ironically, it is this "recognition" that has " helped" to expose Moses' personal weaknesses. Moses is a "prophet" only in so far as he has, like other local "prophets", successfully developed the capacity to deceive his people. By his constant "going in and coming out" — Aluko's deliberately confused version of "co.ning and going" — he has helped to turn a confused political situation into an explosive one.

Aluko's works deserve better critical notice than they have had so far. For, as Hough has pointed out:

> great novelists, like great painters, are created today by advertising and a rigged market. It will in the future require more faith than it did in the past to trust to the common consent of mankind.[33]

Aluko's distinctive contribution to the Nigerian novel is the great variety of English which he uses appropriately in the various situations he develops. As this discussion has shown, his interest in the problems of communication covers a much wider range of linguistic activities than one finds in many another Nigerian novelist. His technical sophistication in the matter of handling language is shown in his deliberate use of cliches and hackneyed expressions to dramatize his very critical attitude to Yoruba culture.

Again, as we move from the first novel to the last, we observe a growing sophistication in Aluko's approach to his writings. In the first two novels, satire is directed in a fairly broad, though effective, way at individuals of a basically simple kind. In the last two, though the intention remains satirical, Aluko is more concerned with the complicities of mental states. For example, Titus in *Kinsman and Foreman*, emerges as a strong character because of his clear mental perception of his total environment. One reason we do not quickly notice Moses' psychological development in *Chief the Honourable Minister* is that it is his attitude to things which changes first. It is only later that this change affects his actions. Aluko's works draw attention not only to the foibles and weaknesses in society but also to the attitudes which must be changed if society must improve. To this extent, they are an important contribution

---

[33] Graham Hough, *An Essay on Criticism* (London, 1966), p.173.

deserving of better recognition than they have received up to now. The link they establish between tradition and modern life frequently exercises and sometimes extends our knowledge of the condition of man in society.

CHAPTER 6
VARIETIES OF ENGLISH IN NKEM NWANKWO'S NOVELS*

I.

In any serious consideration of the novel form, one soon discovers how central an issue is the problem of language. The problem becomes particularly acute in a second language literature, such as we are concerned with in this article. An attempt is made to show how competence in the use of language, affects our evaluation of Nwankwo's works. Examples are given to show how crucial to the author effective co.nmunication is, and how any display of lack of creative intelligence usually results in failure of communication. It is against this background of its importance to meaning that the language of Nkem Nwankwo will be considered. Attention concentrated on his first two novels, especially the second and the areas in which language facilitates or impedes meaning are highlighted.

A writer's language is a mirror held up to his personality and his particular circumstances. It is through the use of language that he reflects his individual awareness of a given situation. What are the particular values Nwankwo is upholding or opposing in each novel? And what is his attitude to them? What varieties of English work best with Nwankwo, on what occasions and for what purpose? Attention is given the whole problem of appropriateness which, following Gumperz and Hymes, is defined as "a specification of what kinds of things to say in what message forms to what kinds of people and in what kinds of situations?"[1]

II.

The point of view is now fairly well accepted that for English to express adequately the way of life of a different culture, it must

---

*First published in *Varieties and Functions of English in Nigeria*, edited by Ebo Ubahakwe, AUP and NESA, 1979, pp. 54—76.
[1] Gumperz and Hymes, "The Ethnography of Communication," *American Anthropologist* 66, 1964 quoted in Abiodun Adetugbo, "Appropriateness and Nigerian English" (Unpublished Manuscript, 1978), p. 1.

endure some internal structural changes.[2] Nigerian novelists, who use English as their creative medium, do so in the consciousness of the fact that they are presenting a Nigerian experience. It is in an attempt to apply English to widely varying local situations that we have varieties of English in the Nigerian novel. It might therefore, be useful for a start to identify what varieties at present exist and attempt later to find out how each of these affects Nwankwo's works.[3]

The first variety of English occurs where the writer's language is closely tied to that of his mother tongue. Usually, this style of writing goes with a near uncritical total acceptance of the culture involved. What the author does, in this case, is to think first in his mother tongue and then transliterate into English. This is the method for which Okara and Tutuola have become famous. It will be referred to in this work as Variety One. This Variety is consciously adopted in the case of Okara, but it is brought about by unavoidable circumstances in the case of Tutuola. Many critics have commented on these linguistic innovations.[4] Not always have these experiments been put in the right perspective and the authors given due credit for their inventiveness. What is usually stressed is the non-English qualities of this variety. What ought to have been emphasized is that language is part of what is created in Tutuola and Okara. Without their experimentation with language, these two would not have been the great authors they are today.

The present writer cannot find anything wrong with an author remaining close to his linguistic roots, if the circumstances demand it. Many Nigerian novelists do this to good effect. T. M. Aluko is a case in point. The influence of Yoruba reveals itself in Aluko's works in many ways. To start with, Yoruba words are used whenever the author considers it appropriate to do so. So we have words like "wahala", "oga", "shekere" and "buba". Many of these words are not important for a correct assessment of the way the novels

---

[2] See, for example, Chinua Achebe, "The Role of the Writer in a New Nation" press, J. ed. *Commonwealth Literature* (London, 1965) and Onwubu C., "Language and Literature: Transliteration in Neo-African Literature," *West African Journal of Modern Languages* 2, 1976, pp. 45–54.

[3] E. N. Obiechina also attempts some categorization in "Variety Differentiation in English Usage," *Journal of the Nigeria English Studies Association,* Vol. 6, No. 1, pp. 77–94.

[4] See, for example, A. Afolayan, "Amos Tutuola: Language and Sources," *Journal of the Nigeria English Studies Association,* 1968, pp. 159–160 and Oladele Taiwo, *Culture and the Nigerian Novel* (London, 1976), pp. 62–73.

work or, in some cases, for the understanding of the sentences in which they occur. For instance, the phrase "o jare" which Aluko often uses amounts to an exclamation in English usage. Although it might be an advantage to know that it carries with it a feeling of disgust, nothing significant is lost if a reader does not know this. Usually, Aluko succeeds in making the meaning of these words clear in their contexts so that the non-Yoruba-speaking reader is not put at a disadvantage. Let us examine one short passage:

> "Pastor, the white men that come to us these days do not know their work properly. The good ones have all left our country," he said sagely, fetching his little snuff-box from the roomy pocket of his agbada.[5]

Aluko might have used the word "gown" if he wanted to, but he insists on the more precise vernacular word, "agbada". However, the non-Yoruba-speaking reader is given enough indication of what the meaning might be. First of all, there is the functional word "fetching" and the very helpful collocation "roomy pocket". "Pocket" leads us to think we are talking of a kind of apparel and "roomy" suggests it is a fairly big one. If the reader does not finally arrive at a correct mental picture of what an "agbada" is, he at least realizes it is a type of big gown. That level of understanding is enough for the purpose of the novel.

But Aluko is not always as successful as this. Some of his problems of communication arise because there are words and concepts in Yoruba which have no equivalents in English — a difficulty experienced by other Nigerian novelists whatever their mother tongue. The word "oba", for example, has no equivalent in the English Language; so Aluko rightly retains it. But his translation of the word "kabiyesi", as "Your Highness", which is the nearest English equivalent, gives a falsified picture of an "oba". The same kind of difficulty arises when Nwankwo uses many Igbo words in a short passage like this:

> The izaga dance is a perilous one, perilous for the dancer. For there are always among the spectators some malevolent dibias who would want to try out the power of a new ogwu by

---

[5] T. M. Aluko, *One Man, One Matchet* (London, 1969), p. 70.

pulling the izaga down. To counter the nsi the izaga needed to be as strong as dried wood.⁶

There are enough Igbo words here to baffle a non-Igbo-speaking reader. To understand this passage, he must know that "izaga" means a masquerader and "dibia", a diviner or medicineman. Even for an Igbo-speaking reader, the distinction between "ogwu" and "nsi" must be a fine one. One means medicine and the other, medicinal attack or charm. The use of the two words here, so close to each other, leads to unnecessary obscurity. But, as we shall see later, Nwankwo usually successfully introduces Igbo words into his text to give it attractive local colour.

The second variety of English (Variety Two) takes after the language of the speaking voice. This, again, is found in many novels but is used mostly by those whose works stand closest to first sources, to the roots of oral tradition. It is the language of folktales, and its main characteristics is the predominance of the habits of speech:

> Amina, I want to say goodbye to you now, for it is my intention to set out before the call to dawn prayer. Now please be patient, you know what the boy is like; whatever he wants to do, if he is not allowed to do it, he will cry, but if he is allowed to do everything that he wants to do, he'll suffer for it in future. The best thing is for you to keep a firm hand on him, and don't bother yourself with thinking, "This boy is not mine"; by God, you and I, we are one, since God has joined us together, and we have been living on terms of friendship.⁷

This is the style of one speaking direct to another. The human voice is lifted, as it were, from the page of the book to our hearing. As we read the passage, we are struck by the rural simplicity and candour of the speaker.

It is the same feeling of directness of speech and familiarity that one finds at the beginning of *The Palm-Wine Drinkard*.

---

⁶Nkem Nwankwo, *Danda* (London, 1970), p. 22.
⁷Tafawa Balewa, *Shaihu Umar* trans. Mervyn Hiskett (London, 1968), pp. 38–9.

I was a palm-wine drinkard since I was a boy of ten years of age. I had no other work more than to drink palm-wine in my life. In those days we did not know other money, except COWRIES, so that everything was very cheap, and my father was the richest man in our town....[8]

Another variety of English, perhaps the most popular and most successful for the creative purpose of Nigerian novelists, is that which merely benefits from the resources of the mother tongue. This will be our Variety Three. Many leading Nigerian fiction writers have adopted this variety – Achebe, Amadi, Aluko – among others. One example of this popular variety takes the form of a dialogue:

"Thank you," said Ezeulu. "Take it to your father to break."
"No," said Akuebue. "I ask you to break it."
"That cannot be. We do not by-pass a man and enter his compound."
"I know that," said Akuebue, "but you see that my hands are full and I am asking you to perform the office for me."
"A man cannot be too busy to break the first kolanut of the day in his own house. So put the yam down; it will not run away."
"But this is not the first kolanut of the day. I have broken several already."
"That may be so, but you did not break them in my presence. The time a man wakes up is his morning."
"All right," said Akuebue. "I shall break it if you say so."
"Indeed I say so. We do not apply an ear-pick to the eye."
Akuebue took the kolanut in his hand and said: "We shall both live," and broke it.[9]

Here we have two elderly members of the society speaking "in character". They speak in proverbs and get to the roots of the local culture in their conversation. Although the original speech is in Igbo, the English version is made to retain the flavour of the original.

---

[8] Amos Tutuola, *The Palm-Wine Drinkard* (London, 1952), p. 7.
[9] Chinua Achebe, *Arrow of God* (A.W.S., London, 1974), p. 138.

This variety also abounds in narratives:

> Six months after the start of negotiations, Ahurole was being escorted finally to her husband's house. It was a pace-making marriage. The normal period of negotiations was a year, but Wigwe had rushed things. Each time Wagbara pointed out that a hen cannot lay eggs and hatch them on the same day, Wigwe had countered by saying that the slow-footed always fail in battle. And so Ahurole was home in six months.[10]

The fourth variety of English tends to be extremely formal and difficult. The content remains African, but, for the most part, there is nothing particularly African in the expression. This variety puts the future of the African novel in great doubt and, for the present, ignores the local audience capable of interpreting African writings. It cannot, therefore, help to popularize the Nigerian novel and make it an instrument of social change. The degree of stylization and sophistication which this variety of English requires is questionable both from the point of view of appropriateness and appeal. A few examples are required to establish the point made here:

> The rains of May become in July slit arteries of the sacrificial bull, a million bleeding punctures of the sky-bull hidden in convulsive cloud humps, blacks, overfed for this one vent, nourished on horizon tops of endless choice gazing, distant beyond giraffe reach. Some competition there is below, as bridges yield right of way to lorries packed to the running-board, and the wet tar spin mirages of unspeed-limits to heroic cars and cargoes find a haven below the precipice. The blood of earth-dwellers mingles with blanched streams of the mocking bull, and flows into currents eternally below earth.[11]

This variety, our Variety Four, is sometimes characterised by empty sloganizing, and journalistic English such as we have here:

---

[10] Elechi Amadi, *The Concubine* (A.W.S., London, 1966), p. 168.
[11] Wole Soyinka, *The Interpreters* (London, 1965), p. 155.

There had never been a mayor in the West African city and now the first one was to be an African. It was a great triumph for the S.G.N. Party. The West African Sensation had been working hard on the elections with such leaders as:

WHO WILL BE MAYOR?
CHOICE OF MAYOR CAUSES SPLIT IN SELF-GOVERNMENT NOW PARTY.
TIME TO REDEEM ELECTION PROMISES.
REALIZATION PARTY THROWS BOMBSHELL.
NATURAL RULERS AND THE NEW CONSTITUTION.

Sango found himself with less and less work to do. Lately, he had developed a habit of leaving the office for longer than he should, searching for a place of his own, and a place for his band. Money was the limiting consideration. They were asking for too much, and he had very little.[12]

The fifth variety — Pidgin English — is a more hopeful medium of expression, with great creative potential. It is true that this potential has not been fully utilized, not even in the Onitsha Market type of literature. It is equally true that writers of distinction like Achebe, Soyinka, Ekwensi, Aig-Imoukhuede, to mention a few, have used Pidgin English effectively in their works. It is now accepted as a distinct variety which can be judiciously used to achieve a correlation between theme, character and situation. The problem arises when, as in Miss Ulasi's works, the medium is employed in a manner which is unconvincing and therefore destroys the basis of effective characterisation. This variety has been extensively discussed elsewhere by this writer and other critics and should not therefore delay us here.[13] But there is need to mention it here because it is established as Variety Five for the purpose of this paper.

III.

Having now established the five broad varieties of English, we

---

[12] Cyprian Ekwensi, *People of the City* (A.W.S. London, 1963), p. 111.
[13] See, for example, Taiwo, *op. cit.*, pp. 48–53 and *The Women Novelists of West Africa* (Unpublished Manuscript, 1978), pp. 5–6; Obiechina, *op. cit.*; Theo Vincent, "Register in Achebe", *Journal of the Nigeria English Studies Association*, Vol. 6, No. 1, pp. 95–106.

must proceed to discuss how relevantly these are featured in Nwankwo's novels and with what result.¹⁴ There can be little doubt about Nwankwo's success with linguistic appropriateness in *Danda*. He usually adopts the third variety of English, that is, the form of prose which recognizes the fundamentals of Igbo language, idiom, sound and flow without rudely shocking the basic English sentence pattern.

> The scorch season was dying. The happiest time of the year, the season for feasts, when men and women laughed with all their teeth and little boys, their mouths oily oily, ran about the lanes blowing the crops of chicken to make balloons. In a few days the rain season would come and bring with it a ceaseless round of labour. And men would leave their homes with the first cry of the cock and would not return until the chicken came back to roost. Already the bushes were on fire and the acrid smell of burning permeated the earth.¹⁵

Many features of Nwankwo's prose style are in evidence here. "The scorch season was dying" is an apt, poetic description of the end of the dry season. "Scorch" brings out forcefully the intensity of the heat, and "dying" significantly conveys the idea of a season which will soon pass into oblivion. The Igbo figures of speech in the next sentence are transliterated into English, in a way which avoids distorting the basic sentence structure — "men and women laughed *with all their teeth*", "little boys *their mouths oily, oily*". The author's easy but firm control of English and the individual quality of his prose reveal themselves in expressions like" a ceaseless round of labour", "the first *cry* of the cock", "*bushes* were on fire", "acrid smell of burning *permeated* the earth." Particularly striking are the flow of ideas and the skillful ordering of sentences which result in a convincing description of the activities marking the end of "the scorch season".

Nwankwo's prose reflects the linguistic characteristics of L1 in other ways:

---

¹⁴ Page references are to the following editions of Nwankwo's two novels: *Danda* (London, 1964); *My Mercedes is Bigger Than Yours* (A.W.S. London, 1975).
¹⁵ *Danda*, p. 81.

Araba waited for him to finish and then said: "People in your age group are doing things, marrying, begetting children, buying *land-boats*. What have you done?"
"Time is still big," said Danda...
"And you are not to appear in the ebe for *six moons.*"
"Impossible." Danda thought for a moment, finished the second cup he had been carrying and continued: "I will attend the next dance."
"It is not wise," said Okelekwu. "A man who is sensible does not, open-eyed, jump into the fire."
"I will attend the next dance," Danda said again.
Araba snuffed, sighed, and said: "It is when a dog, hungers for death that it begins to eat sand."[16]

Araba's anxiety about his son's apparent lack of progress is expressed in a simple and homely language which relies on L1 for its effectiveness. "Land-boats" (for cars) and "six moons" (for six months) are direct influences of L1; "ebe" (village square) is an Igbo word left untranslated in the text. It is one of several such words which constantly remind the reader of the cultural background against which the story is written. "Time is still big" is another transliteration from Igbo which is very appropriate in the context. We find in this passage examples of proverbs used to transmit to the young the wisdom of the ancients. The purpose here is didactic — to get Danda to see reason and respect traditional authority.

The structure of the book gives the novelist an ample opportunity to introduce many of the varieties of English into his work. Danda is his central character who is made to react with both old and new. Through him the established traditional order and Christianity are exposed in turn, and Danda emerges triumphant.

Nwankwo's method is to use Danda's antics to present a society which is quietly undergoing social change. Danda's quips and abundant vitality prevent the villagers from noticing the strains and tensions which are already disturbing the apparently smooth surface of communal life. The values of the society to which change is coming are well documented in the appropriate variety of English:

The quantity of feathers had come to be an index of a man's

---

[16] *Ibid.*, pp. 36–7 (my italics).

standing in the community. The more of it there was the more the number of chickens he could afford to kill and therefore the greater his wealth would be taken to be.[17]

Araba's claims to recognition are based on:

> A long barn, ten women, an obi of which much noise was made. Araba was known too to have always been a fighter for Aniocha and Uwadiegwu. Finally and most important of all, he had taken the ozo before anybody alive.[18]

These are the values which Danda rejects and seeks to undermine.

It is also in the appropriate third variety that the elders discuss matters which concern the welfare of the society, as we have in these passages:

> "When I spoke to him he said that the ngwu agelega was his father's."
> "No man can hold on to what Danda says. What Danda says has neither head nor tail."
> There was laughter.
> "It does not amuse me!" roared the Ikolo man. "It is long since Danda began pouring sand into our eyes."
> "But is the ngwu agelega his or his father's? We want to know...."
> "Araba," he said to the big-headed ozo. "Is the ngwu agelega yours?"
> Araba stirred and said calmly: "This is a question for Danda himself. I haven't been home to know whether the ngwu agelega he carried is mine or his."
> "Why should he have one? Is he an ozo man?"[19]

Danda continually asserts his individualism. His use of the ngwu agelega (ozo staff) without being an ozo is a serious offence, but he gets away with it, as with his other breaches of custom. He comes to be accepted as an enigma in society. By reconciling themselves

---

[17] *Ibid.*, p. 17.
[18] *Ibid.*, p. 45.
[19] *Ibid.*, p. 29.

to Danda's antics and failing to punish his abuse of tradition, the people are unconsciously adjusting to the changes which will inevitably overtake them. His antics and quips serve only as the thin end of the wedge which rips society apart to make way for a new order.

The novelist's sense of humour is everywhere in evidence in this passage in which he shows great sensitivity in the use of the designated Varieties Two and Three:

> "My voice is low. The proverb says that the word biko (please) never leads to a quarrel."
> "True! True!"
> "If I have wronged you, my knees are on the ground. After all I am your son and a father doesn't bear ill-will against his own son for long."
> "No! No!"
> "If a man cooks for the community, the community will eat it all. But if the community cooks for a single person he cannot eat the cooking."
> "Say no more!" roared the umunna, scrambling for their cups.
> "You have come like a man," said Nwafo Ugo.
> The matter of the ofo was again shelved....[20]

Araba's plea for pardon to the umunna is made in moving prose, and in a manner which deserves sympathetic response — "my voice is low". But no action is taken at the meeting because, with food and drinks provided in abundance, the elders, "scrambling for their cups" completely forget the important purpose of their meeting, as the last sentence of the passage shows. Elders who behave in this way have no moral right to lead others and only help to bring into disrepute the traditional order which they represent.

It is through the use of Igbo words and proverbs, the reflection of Igbo idioms of speech in his prose that Nwankwo achieves his creative purpose in this novel. The ultimate goal is to change society with its limits and prescriptions on individual liberty into a more open, and therefore more democratic, community in which the freedom of speech and action is guaranteed. We recognize something of this new order in Danda, when he makes his last dramatic appearance in the novel:

---

[20] *Ibid.*, pp. 158–59.

"Son of our fathers," said Nwokeke, *his eyes laughing*,
"Where do you spring up from?"

"Did they tell you, your father's house is crumbling?" bawled Nwora Otankpa.

"Leave it to me," said Danda. "I have come to take possession of my obi and nothing will crumble."

In the face of such assurance there was nothing more to be said.

"Let's hear the drummers then," said Nwokeke. "*The day is going home slowly, slowly.*"

The drummers found a place, tuned up their instruments and began to play.

Danda stood staring at them with bright-keen eyes, *drinking in their tunes*. In a moment they began to work on him. The calves of his legs shook, his whole body simmered with excitement. He went mad.

"My father bore me well, my chi created me well."[21]

Here is Danda, the gay, high-spirited village clown, in his greatest mo.nent of triumph. He is the harbinger of a new era in which life will be less circumscribed by taboos and rituals, and individual self-expression will not be hampered by tradition.

IV.

While *Danda* ends on a note of triumph for the individual, the message of *My Mercedes is Bigger Than Yours* (*My Mercedes*, for short) is one of despair and uncertainty. *Danda* has been mostly witty and humorous, *My Mercedes* is bitterly satirical. This must be partly responsible for the change in Nwankwo's style and approach. A new subject calls for an entirely different treatment, and a new kind of material calls for a different kind of language. This may be part of the thinking behind the creation of *My Mercedes*. Although a fresh approach can always be justified, there is no reason why this should be less attractive than the previous one. *My Mercedes*, coming more than ten years after *Danda*, must have come to many critics as a disappointment.

---

[21] *Ibid.*, p. 201 (my italics).

One does not find the correlation between theme, language and situation which makes *Danda* so attractive. The material of *My Mercedes* is thin on the ground and hardly deserves the kind of attention given to it by the author. The reader is offered little information by way of background to the events, to which he is suddenly introduced. Onuma is important only because he possesses a jaguar car. This car is wrecked early in the story and the rest of the narration is devoted to the disastrous effect of this accident on Onuma. Even if one accepts that the jaguar car, with all that it stands for socially and politically, may bring about these devastating consequences, it will still be difficult to justify the novelist's haphazard selection of details, especially towards the end of the novel. On this occasion, Nwankwo stretches the reader's imagination too far. One wonders whether he is not now writing with diminished artistic talent.

Most of the events of this novel take place in the village, yet the author decides to use highly formalised language for the most part. This is how the author comments on the situation created by the loss of the jaguar car.

> It was therefore to a despairing mother and an alarmed father that Onuma explained the situation. He was a little annoyed with their tragic mien although he himself had been driven almost crazy when he thought the car was gone. So he laboured to play down the extent of the accident. He tried to convince them that it was only a matter of time before the car would be back on the road. Udumezue nodded with sage relief. But it was left to the mother to sum it up in her woman's stoical way.[22]

Authorial comments on an intimate situation involving son and parents hardly call for such a formal language. This falls within Variety Four which, as we have pointed out, does more harm than good to African Literature.

There are other linguistic lapses in the novel, some of them amounting to an artistic failure on the part of the author. We have time for only a few examples:

---

[22] *My Mercedes is Bigger Than Yours*, p. 64.

> Koko clammed up at once. His expansive manner gave way to a distracted business; the black moist eyes of a practised womaniser clouded, he bent his handsome bushy brows in a painful attempt at concentration on a big ledger and in a changed voice reminded Onuma of a long-standing credit.[23]

The occasion here hardly calls for a grandiloquent language. The author is giving us Koko's reaction to Onuma's enquiry about the possibility of a loan to help him overcome his financial difficulties. This passage occurs in the middle of what appears to be a familiar conversation between two friends. The language is therefore inappropriate. True, the language of a narrative may be different from that of a dialogue, but unnecessary formality in any part of a book should be avoided in the author's interest.

> Once upon a time a young man was savouring the pleasures of a new car. He was thinking that there were really occasions when a car seemed to drive itself as it were, seemed to respond to some remote stimulus independent of the driver. It had its moments of cursedness, of course, when it whined and snorted for no particular reason, then there were moments of heavenly smoothness when it floated on the crest of some intangible wave.[24]

This is how the novel starts and Nwankwo intimates us that this work will be dominated by formal English. Otherwise, this might be considered a good beginning. It introduces us without delay to the two most important entities in the story — Onuma, "a young man" and the car. The word "wave" which occurs in this passage and in other parts of the novel is central to the novel's preoccupation. Onuma benefits maximally from the possession of a car and for some time rides on a "wave" of popularity, debasing himself in the process. He forgets that a car is a perishable article. When he loses his car, he falls from glory, as it were. This fall is made very sudden and therefore loses part of its impact. But once it takes place, he enters a new and unpleasant phase in his life. A "wave" of strange experiences carry him to his bitter end.

---

[23] *Ibid.*, p. 83.
[24] *Ibid.*, p. 1.

The formal language of the novel can occasionally be justified by the need to recapture in print the spirit of a man whose only obsession in life is the possession of a big car:

> An enormous orgastic excitement coursed through Onuma's body, causing him goose pimples of pleasure. Mentally he savoured the flanks and public softness of this beaµtiful new mistress. Then he began to ride her and she moved with lovely art and sensuous obedience, moaning softly, giving him everything, denying him nothing. He rode on and on, forcing her through the most erotic paces, swinging her, bending her, licking her, swimming in her. Tears of joy and gratitude streamed down his face. He went on and on, directionless. He was not going to stop, ever.[25]

Onuma gets hold of another car after a long spell of being without one, and is naturally excited by it.

It is not in every part that the language of the book is formal. Nwankwo uses nearly all the other designated Varieties of English, and often with good artistic results:

> Magic laughed incredulously. "So that is the way these things are done nowadays. We work and toil here for nothing and they think they can order us about.... Well go and tell your Eze...!"
>
> The Albino had been staring at Magic while he made this speech. At last, unable to contain himself any more he fell on the rebel. "You have come again. What do you know about the party? Are you the Eze? If the Eze wants to make this man sheaman who are you to say no?... Do you know book? Have you been to univaiti? Are you not a village blockhead like all of us?"
>
> "I am not a village blockhead. You mistake the man you are talking with."
>
> "Oh yes, we know all about your travels but you are still a Yokel, so there!"[26]

---

[25] *Ibid.*, p. 171.
[26] *Ibid.*, p. 137.

This reminds one of many of such passages in *Danda*. By the use of such variant spellings like "sheaman", "univaiti" and such expressions like

> "So that is the way these things are done nowadays."
> "You have come again."
> "Do you know book?"

the novelists lends local colour to his writing and exploits in a beneficial manner the resources of the Igbo language.

Other passages in the narrative and dialogue parts of the book confirm the novelist's judicious use of Varieties One to Three:

> "Ada, come here. Go to Mbammili. Tell my brother Okike that my face is full of shame. They know that my son Onuma is coming home today and none of them has done anything." She thought a bit. "Tell them that Udemezue wants them all to come later in the evening"
> "Yes mother."
> "And tell my brother's son, Nweze, to come now quickly, eh?"
> "Yes mother."
> The small girl scrambled away but just as she reached the gate the woman shouted: "And listen, Ogoli must not come, do you hear?"
> "Yes mother," said the girl, disappearing through the gate. Oliaku knew that Ogoli would come.[27]

The only other variety of English used in *My Mercedes* — our fifth variety — is Pidgin English (Pidgin). The quality of the writer's Pidgin is high and is limited to only relevant situations. So it does not distract the attention of the reader whose ears are attuned to good Pidgin, as is the case with some Nigerian novels.[28] What we have in this novel is fluent standard Pidgin which reveals always great sensitivity to a developing situation.

---

[27] *Ibid.*, p. 3.
[28] See, for example, Miss Ulasi's first two novels:
  1. *Many Thing You No Understand* (London, 1970).
  2. *Many Thing Begin for Change* (London, 1971).

"Wetin?" he growled.
"Can I see the manager?"
"We no get manager here. Wetin you want?"
"I want a salvage car."
"Salvage car? No be manager you say you want?"
"Well, can I see the manager?"
"Can I see the manager now?" asked Onuma.
"This is the engineer," said the gateman severely.[29]

In this passage, Pidgin is used appropriately for character delineation. It is used to differentiate between two classes of people as we also have in this other passage:

"Big man for noting abi you no see? This place na bus stop" one shouted.
"No Minam. E tink say na only im wey sabi drive Citroen." grumbled another.
"Big man debtor, why you no commot?"[30]

Pidgin is used here in the right situation to expose to ridicule Onuma's bad driving and to reveal some in-built antagonism between the rich and the poor, between those who ride in big cars and those who walk on foot.

V.

We have identified five varieties of English and aplied these, as appropriate, to the works of Nwankwo. An analysis has shown that the novelist uses the first variety sparingly. This is just as well because a writer who relies excessively on a word-for-word transliteration of his mother tongue to English cannot hope to achieve local acclaim or help in the modernization of African Literature in English.

We find that Nwankwo uses Varieties Two and Three a great deal, and this is what is mainly responsible for the success of *Danda*. These varieties, especially Variety Three, have many advantages.

---

[29] *My Mercedes is Bigger Than Yours*, p. 89.
[30] *Ibid.*, p. 67.

They help the novelist produce an illusion of reality through the selection of details from ordinary life. They give local colour to the work and have been largely responsible for the experimentation in form and language which one finds in the Nigerian novel. These varieties, along with Pidgin English, are used to the best effect by Nwankwo. They contain the seed of future development and will help to establish African Literature in English in its own right. But the ultimate goal must be kept in sight. For, as I have said elsewhere, "the challenge of our time therefore is to help to encourage, the growth of a literature which is not only indigenous to Africa but is also good enough to stand comparison with the literatures of other parts of the world."[31]

We find that Variety Four cannot in any way help this process. If anything, it will retard the growth of the African novel and prevent it from having a distinct character of its own. As has been demonstrated already, what makes Nwankwo's second novel less successful than the first is the fact that the work is dominated by this variety which is usually too formal for the author's purpose. This variety tends to remove part of the distinctive nature of African literature and limit the amount of experimentation that can take place. No wonder, Gakwandi finds that:

> Compared with poetry and drama the African novel has been shy of experiment. The best African poets have not written odes, elegies and sonnets. They have invented new models to embody their reactions to modern life.... By contrast, the leading African novelists have been satisfied with employing the techniques developed by European realism and have used them to comment upon African experience. Local colour is there — in Achebe, Laye, Ngugi and Oyono — but the basic form remains unaltered.[32]

One may not agree completely with Gakwandi. But there can be no doubt that it is only through the use of the appropriate Varieties of English in the treatment of local or universalized situations that the African novel can command more respect than it does at the moment.

---

[31] Oladele Taiwo, *An Introduction to West African Literature* (London, 1967), p. 181.
[32] Arthur Gakwandi, *The Novel and Contemporary Experience in Africa* (London, 1977), p. 127.

CHAPTER 7
THE USE OF COMEDY IN NIGERIAN FICTION*

I.

The use of comedy in Nigerian fiction is closely connected with the factors which provided the motivation for African writing in English in the first place. The colonial situation which encouraged the belief in the superiority of one race over another constituted a major factor. Therefore, comedy often arises in Nigerian fiction, especially in the earlier books, from the behaviour of colonial political officers who usually insist on the superiority of their culture and way of life. It is necessary to go in some detail into the origins of these unfounded European beliefs before examining, how, through the use of comedy, the Nigerian novelists have reacted to the cultural and historical environment in which they found themselves.

For a long time in history, Africa was widely misrepresented abroad. When eventually the "Dark Continent" was penetrated, travellers and missionaries came out with dreadful stories — more imaginary than true — of human sacrifice, cannibalism, intertribal wars and abject poverty. According to Eldred Jones in *Othello's Countrymen*, the two main sources of Englishmen's knowledge of Africa in the sixteenth century were "the tales of the ancients as popularized by translations, and the contemporary accounts of sailors who had themselves seen Africa".[1] But he is quick to add that these accounts were a mixture of fact and fiction.

This stock image was carried into the colonial period and was, in fact, used as a justification for colonialism. Colonial administrators helped for the most part to perpetuate this image. G. D. Killam in his *Africa in English Fiction* gives as one of many examples the case of George Alfred Henty, a single-minded exponent of imperialism and its uncritical supporter. As a colonial administrator, he gave inaccurate and largely imaginary accounts of Africa. His attitude

---
*First published in *The Literary Half-Yearly* (Mysore, India) XV/2, July 1974, pp. 107–120.
[1] Eldred Jones, *Othello's Countrymen*, 1965, p. 1.

was paternalistic in an age which took African inferiority for granted and therefore, readily accepted the view that Africans.

> ... are just like children .... They are always either laughing or quarrelling. They are good-natured and passionate, indolent, but will work hard for a time; clever up to a certain point, densely stupid beyond. The intelligence of an average negro is about equal to that of a European child of ten years old. They are absolutely without originality, absolutely without inventive power. Living among white men, their imitative faculties enable them to attain a considerable amount of civilization. Left alone to their own devices they retrograde into a state little above their native savagery.[2]

Thus, started a tradition of writing during the colonial era which had the effect of popularizing the notion of British superiority and duty to the less fortunate, almost helpless, people of Africa. As Killam reports, nearly all the novels in this tradition, if novels they may be called, initially failed to present believable portraits of Africans.

The literary pretensions of the novels of this early period and the image of Africa they project have undoubtedly affected the consciousness of Nigerian novelists a great deal. Consequently, a lot of creative attention has been devoted to the colonial situation in Nigerian fiction. The British administrator is usually presented as a local representative of a distant tyrannical power, a man, who, because of his ignorance of local customs, traditions and beliefs, provides in his actions a wide scope for wit and humour, the two components of comedy. It is true that this comedy is often tolerant and balanced, critical yet sympathetic to officials who, after all, may be making a desperate effort to understand the society in which they find themselves.

Achebe's work provides many examples of this phenomenon. The District Commissioner at the end of *Things Fall Apart*, seems to be just as out of touch with the true feelings of Umuofia as Okonkwo, and he is hardly the type of administrator needed at this crucial time to bring home to Umuofians the advantages to be derived from British Administration. First, through a combination

---

[2] George Henty, *By Sheer Pluck*, P. 118 quoted in G.D. Killam, *Africa in English Fiction 1874–1939*, Ibadan, 1968, p. 21.

of treachery and naked show of power he arrests the six leaders of the people, offers them no opportunity to defend themselves and then proceeds to harangue them in a speech which is highly provocative. He misses the whole significance of the death of Okonkwo—Obierika's explanation leaves no impression on him. To him the dangling body of Okonkwo constitutes "undignified details", only good enough to be relegated to a paragraph in a book he is planning to write:

> The story of this man who had killed a messenger and hanged himself would make interesting reading. One could almost write a whole chapter on him. Perhaps not a whole chapter but a reasonable paragraph, at any rate. There was so much else to include, and one must be firm in cutting out details.³

This District Commissioner not only exceeds his mandate in his dealings with the people but displays his ignorance of the gravity of the situation so energetically that he becomes ridiculous in his actions and thought. His abnormalities of character are employed to isolate him from his environment.

Clarke, the political officer in *Arrow of God* is put in a similar laughable situation. He is made to adopt an attitude of superiority to the people. His "lecture" to Ezeulu reveals a basic flaw in his character, which the novelist magnifies for comic effect.

> After that he calmed down and spoke about the benefits of the British Administration. Clarke had not wanted to deliver this lecture which he would have called complacent if somebody else had spoken it. But he could not help himself. Confronted with the proud inattention of this fetish priest whom they were about to do a great favour by elevating him above his fellows and who, instead of gratitude, returned scorn, Clarke did not know what else to say. The more he spoke the more he became angry.⁴

This passage touches on some of the problems of Indirect Rule, especially the reasons for its failure among the Igbo. It also shows

---

³*Things Fall Apart*, 1969, p. 187.
⁴*Arrow of God*, 1967, p. 215.

that Ezeulu's fate is intimately tied up with the colonial situation. Achebe's language and the setting, reflect the conflict of ideas and beliefs which are essential features of such a situation. At one end of the conflict, as described in this passage, is Ezeulu as the representative of his people, at the other end, is Clarke as the representative of the local Administration. The importance of this kind of setting lies in the way it dramatizes the social and political gulf which separates the two. Clarke's actions only widen this gulf further. His "complacent" lecture can only have the same type of disastrous effect which the "lecture" of the District Commissioner in *Things Fall Apart* has on the leaders of Umuofia. Such lectures only compel the "proud inattention" of arrogant men like Ezeulu and shown how unintentionally a political officer can lend himself to comedy.

Often comedy is centred on colonial organizations like the European Club in *No Longer at Ease* or off-shoots of European life like Christianity. In Achebe's treatment of the Club, its aim and practice are shown to be unimportant mainly through the inane language of its members:

"Hello, Peter. Hello, Bill."
"Hello."
"Hello."
"May I join you?"
"Certainly."
"Most certainly. What are you drinking, Beer? Right. Steward. One beer for this master."
"What kind, sir?"
"Heineken."
"Yes, sir."[5]

This sort of language does look inane, especially when taken out of context. But, as we all know, people who are not "inane" at all very often do make verbal exchanges of this sort, in all kinds of situations, for life cannot be lived at a consistent level of verbal intensity. Achebe's purpose is no doubt to show why the European Club comes to mean nothing to Obi in the face of more pressing problems. However, in the process, we have what amounts to comedy of manners.

---

[5]*No Longer at Ease*, 1969, p. 4.

II.

Comedy is not only used by Nigerian novelists to reflect the people's resentment of colonialism. In those works which attempt to dramatise the realities and dilemmas of Nigerian life, comedy is used to underline a certain lack of seriousness in the national character — a growing tendency which reached its climax during the last civil war, the tendency to make light of serious issues and to dance, wine and womanise even in the face of death. This gaiety of life, this over-confidence bordering on irresponsibility, provides a lot of material for the writer of comedy. Occasionally, as is the case with Ogidi in *Wind Versus Polygamy*, certain selected characteristics, like pride and material success, are exaggerated for comic effect. Ogidi is notable only for his mannerisms — "Yeah", "very embarrassing" — and the ridiculous habit of wiping his face with five-pound notes — "I'm always making this mistake, wiping my face with fivers."[6] He makes a fool of himself by believing he can buy Elina with money or win her affection by an ostentatious display of wealth. He realizes his folly too late. Ogidi's contribution to the novel is the humour he provides by his antics. He is not the sort of character through whom any modern idea like monogamy or a better standard of living is likely to gain acceptance.

The popular pamphlets, usually referred to as Onitsha Market Literature, concern themselves with surface appearances, and hardly ever consider underlying causes. Because they attempt only to reproduce the problems and social realities of life, they are often impregnated with comic scenes. Onitsha Market Literature has been studied intensively in recent years. The most illuminating study has come from Dr. Emmanuel Obiechina, who has made a detailed comparison of the works of pamphlet authors with those of intellectual writers.[7] According to him:

> A comparison of works by the two groups of authors shows that in terms of their reflection of things as they actually are, we are likely to find the pamphleteers much nearer to the

---

[6] Obi Egbuna, *Wind versus Polygamy*, 1964, p. 45.
[7] See the two recent publications by Dr. Obiechina:
(a) *Literature for the Masses*, Enugu, 1971.
(b) *Onitsha Market Literature*, 1972.

experience of most ordinary people than the sophisticated authors. They reflect the problems and crises of contemporary life in all their rawness. By the time these have undergone intellectual digestion in the quality works of the intellectual authors, a certain amount of blood must have been lost from the life that reappears.[8]

Obiechina also tells us why pamphlets are so thoroughly comic in their presentation of material:

> In the treatment of its major themes and interests, the Onitsha pamphlet Literature retains its popular quality of simplicity and lightness. Even while dealing with what might appear the most serious subjects, its approach is hardly ever solemn. The desire to entertain and amuse is always paramount in the pamphlets. The typical pamphlet author paints his picture with a light comic brush. That is why the pamphlet scene is teeming with comic, ridiculous and grotesque characters and incidents.[9]

This is not to suggest that only Pamphlet Literature can be amusing. Intellectual writers are occasionally extremely witty. One of the most humorous books in Nigerian Fiction is *Danda*, in which the author uses Danda, a playboy kind of fellow, to indicate the need for social change. On the face of it, Danda is a man of shiftless irresponsibility. He is a picaroon whose knavery involves him in adventures which take him from one social class to another, a social parasite who often successfully exploits men and women in more elevated positions. Like Amadi's Wakiri, he is the village clown, who escapes being taken to task for his misconduct because of an assumed lack of seriousness. Danda makes up for any personal defects, and the inconvenience caused others, by entertaining the villagers with his antics, singing and dancing. His jokes endear him to all the people:

> If there is a man to whom what is good is not good let him dig his own grave and see how he likes it.[10]

---

[8] *Literature for the Masses*, p. 81.
[9] *Ibid.*, p. 7.
[10] Nkem Nwankwo, *Danda*, 1970, p. 22. All page references are to this edition.

If there is any one to whom what is good is not good let him embrace the thorn tree and see how he likes it.[11]

(to boys): When your father quarrels with your mother take the part of the father for he owns the home. (to girls): Don't worry your heads over husbands; I will find them for you.[12]

(to a group of girls singing): All the men love you. If there is any man who doesn't love you let him put his head in the fire and see how he likes it.[13]

Some people say that Danda is a tortoise, others that he is mad. I am not mad, people of our land, but I am not so sure that I am sane. Give us palm wine.[14]

There is also the favourite saying for which he is popular throughout the village: "That which is in the pot should be in the belly."[15]

The villagers become so accustomed to enjoying Danda's jokes and witticisms that they often miss the underlying seriousness of what he says:

"The world is bad nowadays," said Danda. "Let the world be good. Let this Oji cleanse the world. Let it make us friends. May each man have what is due to him. The hawk shall perch and the eagle shall perch. Whichever bird says to the other don't perch let its wings break."[16]

The importance of these remarks, made on a convivial occasion when villagers are treated to so much Oji (wine), is not likely to be fully appreciated. His listeners would no doubt endorse Danda's supplication, "Let this Oji cleanse the world." But, in fact, the type of "cleansing" that he has in mind is one that could destroy all that the villagers hold dear and shake the fabric of society to its very foundation. This difference between Danda and the others is underlined by his wish for the "bad" world to change to "good". In this context Danda is "good", or at least potentially so, and the others

---

[11] *Ibid.*, p. 54.
[12] *Ibid.*, p. 19.
[13] *Ibid.*, p. 83.
[14] *Ibid.*, p. 90.
[15] *Ibid.*, p. 158.
[16] *Ibid.*, p. 13.

are "bad". The plea for friendship and accommodation, especially as symbolized by the reference to the hawk and the eagle, looks forward to issues that are central to the novel's preoccupation — the confrontation between paganism and Christianity, the numerous encounters between Danda and the ozos. "May each man have what is due to him" is a piece of advice which, if heeded, would have averted the acrimonious dispute between Nwokeke and Araba over the Nwadiegwu ozala, which destroys the unity of the extended family and leads to such an important member as Araba being ostracized from it. So this apparently frivolous speech refers by implication to matters which are of paramount interest to the listeners.

Not only is the reader held contentedly spellbound by Danda's activities, the novelist's sense of humour is also everywhere in evidence. Nwankwo scoffs mildly at man's foibles and employs a method of gentle ridicule to expose the seamy side of village life. There is, for instance, the important meeting of the umunna, to which the whole of Chapter Seven is devoted. In his description of the events at this meeting, Nwankwo shows an eye for detail and evokes to perfection the villagers' delight in long speeches which defeat the purpose of the gathering. The chief participants are introduced in a laughable sort of way: Esili is "a mite of a man with sharp features and a cringing manner."[17] Nwego, the cynic who swears falsely before the Alusi and turns the whole occasion into a farce, is "a gaunt fellow with a goatee; bright, lazy, eyes; who smoked a long slightly charred pipe." The Alusi, the object of the people's fear and the focus of attention at the meeting, is described as "a conelike god dressed in skins, blood and leaves" and his priest, as "a tall lanky man, who carried a twenty-year sore festering in his leg."[18] Of the conduct of those at the meeting, the behaviour of the palm wine tapper is typical:

> "My bottom is hot," he cried. "How long are we going to stay here? People get up and talk and talk as if they were never going to make an end. Is there a law that a man must be long-winded? Is there any alu in being brief? If you have nothing to do, I have. My palms are waiting for me."

---

[17] *Ibid.*, p. 48.
[18] *Ibid.*, p. 60.

The rest of the umunna nodded their heads in support. But the tapster having now cleared the ground, and created sympathy for himself, went ahead and made the longest speech of all.[19]

The reader is not surprised that the meeting ends in a fiasco.

Humour arises at times from the difference between people's estimates of themselves and their real worth, as is the case with Nweke Alusi:

> The poster read
> "Nweke Alusi, native doctor.
> Registered in Nigeria.
> Man-pass-man.
> Come to me for power medicine — to kure madness, hatfelior, "akpu" foming in the maut (eiplezi), venerable diseasis etc.
> Money back if not satisfactri."[20]

The humour here arises from the false claims of this quack herbalist. Alusi's incompetence is displayed on the "poster" for all to see. The illiterate spellings — hatfelior, kure, satisfactri — the mixture of vernacular and English — "akpu" foming in the maut — and the confusion of words — "venerable" for venereal — make the claim of "Man-pass-Man!" laughable. The obscurity which results from his inadequate means of communication may be intended to depict, in some measure, the potential for evil which men like Alusi possess.

Occasionally the humour results from the use of a particular word:

> "She is from Umukrushe."
> "From where?"
> There was a burst of laughter.
> "Okelekwu, my brother, what did you say it was? People of our land wait a moment. Let the name reach the depths of my ear."
> "Umukrushe."
> "Ahai! The names that exist in this world."[21]

---

[19] *Ibid.*, p. 58.
[20] *Ibid.*, p. 52.
[21] *Ibid.*, p. 84.

The word "Umukrushe" sounds extremely funny and fulfils the author's expectation of provoking laughter. The people of Aniocha cannot bring themselves to believe that any such place exists. According to them, "no village has the right to give itself such a name."[22]

Sometimes it is the people's habit of speech which provides the humour Igbo words are made to acquire the force of a deliberate affectation in style:

> "I am afraid of death, the way it attacks.
> No matter how strong a man is, when death comes, chololom! he goes.
> Man is little, with a sound, fium! He dissolves like sand."[23]

"Chololom" and "fium" in their onomatopoeic effect, are funny mannerisms. The author shares with his main character an abiding interest in the pleasantries of village life. It is through a series of humorous situations, in which various aspects of life are ridiculed, that the inadequacy of tradition is presented in this novel.

III.

In recent years, novels have appeared which, in their criticism of society, have tended to lack the tolerant spirit of compromise and accommodation usually associated with comedy. In them, the comic vision has taken a satiric form. Although they often use comic vision has taken a satiric form. Although they often use comedy to achieve their purpose, they point out their lessons sharply and frequently with bitterness. This is not altogether surprising in a society, where there are both well-established rules of behaviour and also rebels who are willing to pit themselves against tradition. One must also reckon with the fast rate at which science, technology and political modernization erode traditional authority. All this provides material for the comic writer and the satirist alike. But because the approach of the satirist can be very sharp and effective, it is he, who has benefited most from the situation. He has raised

---

[22] *Ibid.*, p. 85.
[23] *Ibid.*, p. 152.

comedy to the level of satire and through this medium shown his dissatisfaction with both tradition and modern experience.

This feeling of utter dissatisfaction was first highlighted in modern Nigerian fiction by Cyprian Ekwensi in his creation of Uncle Taiwo in *Jagua Nana*. Satire has since been successfully used as an instrument of social criticism by other Nigerian novelists, notably Soyinka, Okara, Achebe and Aluko. The last two have produced some of the best satires in Nigerian fiction partly because of their essentially critical attitude to indigenous culture. However, a close comparison will reveal that Aluko's attitude to indigenous culture is decidedly more critical than that of Achebe; at least, this is what it would, on immediate response to his novels, appear to be. In Aluko, the treatment of customs and traditions in modern context takes the form of a more consistently sustained satire than one finds in Achebe. One must, however, remember such things as the closing page of *Things Fall Apart*, the dinner party in *Arrow of God*, and almost any chapter of *No Longer at Ease*, not to mention the overall effect of *A Man of the People*. To be sure, the focus of satire in Achebe tends, as the examples cited illustrate, to be that which militates against traditional culture rather than traditional culture in itself. But although one would not think of *Things Fall Apart*, in its overall effect, as a *satirical* novel, the ways in which Achebe expresses an ambivalent attitude towards things which in part he admires in Igbo culture, plainly point to a disposition of mind which is likely to lead to the creation of satirical fiction.

Even readers disposed readily to agree with what has just been said, however, would be justified in making the point that Achebe, even in *A Man of the People* is at least as elegiac as he is satirical. That is to say, *A Man of the People*, very largely depends for its satiric effect upon an elegiac recognition of the greater things in Nigerian culture, however, subject to qualifying scrutiny, that have passed away. Aluko, on the other hand, can strike the reader as being purely satirical from the first novel to the last. This raises for the reader the problem of determining the precise scope and intentions of his satire.

So Aluko must be seen as a writer who, although using comedy for his ends, points out his lessons with greater bitterness than one finds in other Nigerian novels. Most Nigerian novelists use comedy either to take it back on the white man, for historical reasons, or to ridicule certain abnormalities, characters and ideas. Through the use of comedy, they draw attention not only to the foibles and weaknesses in society but also to the attitudes which must be changed if society must improve. To this extent, they perform an essential function which deserves the highest recognition.

CHAPTER 8
DRAMA IN EDUCATION: AN ANALYSIS OF THREE PLAYS*

I.

Drama plays a crucial role at various levels of education. At an early age, it helps the transfer to school of those activities — singing, dancing, play-acting — which the child is already used to at home. These activities are based on "doing" and active participation rather than "listening" and passive reception. This underlines the importance of drama as a teaching method. At every stage in the child's education drama, properly utilised, brings about a desirable change in behaviour and provides critical insight which has been defined as

> A probing beneath the surface, a penetration into the total meaning of text...

Which embraces a number of implied

> meanings, emotional overtones, and symbolism, and such strands as plot, theme, character, mood and moral.[1]

This statement is important in the way it calls attention to the aspects of drama which should be studied in detail, if learning is to become apparent in the changed behaviour of the individual. These considerations are many: there is the problem of the cultural relevance of material and the appropriateness of the mode of expression. Will the material help to integrate the learner with his indigenous culture or will it alienate him from his background? How edifying is the information contained in the passage or material to be taught? Is the mode of expression suitable to the given age and circumstance?

---

*First published in *JNESA* edited by S. O. Onoh.
[1] John Morris, "Creative Reading" in *English Language Teaching* (London, 1961) 26 (IV), pp. 257–261.

Once the teacher has satisfied himself on these matters, he goes ahead to provide the necessary motivation, orders his material in a new and exciting way, breaks his "content" into small, assimilable units for easy presentation and digestion by the learner. He should later test the learner's understanding of the material through a practical application of the principles involved. This is very easy to do in drama. Since in drama the learner uses his mind, body and voice, it is possible to test the material in a concrete manner and see what change there has been in the behaviour of the learner as a result of his recent experience.

In this paper, three plays will be examined in detail in order to determine their suitability for the propagation of drama as a valuable educational medium. The discussion in each case benefits from some of the criteria and considerations mentioned above. Particular attention is paid to the distinctive features of each play, the extent to which it can help develop originality in the learner and provide him with the opportunity of creative imagination which, according to Andrew Weaver," is the key to mental freedom".[2]

II.

The Incorruptible Judge is a short play suitable for use at the lower secondary school.[3] Both the language and theme are appropriate for this level. The theme is meant to enrich the social and cultural experience of the child. The purpose of the work is to a large extent didactic, even though the author in a preface claims that "its primary aim is to entertain." (p. 4). The subject-matter is popular and attractive: A school leaver applies for a job to an Establishment Officer, who demands a bribe of five pounds. Instead of paying up, as many would do, the applicant reports the matter to the police, who arrest the corrupt official and take him to court. He is jailed for three years. This topic cannot but compel the attention of students, who themselves may soon be looking for employment.

---

[2] Andrew Weaver, *The Fundamentals and Forms of Speech* (New York: The Odyssey Press, 1957), p. 373.
[3] D. Olu. Olagoke, *The Incorruptible Judge* (London: Evans, 1962). All page references are to the 1978 edition of the book.

It is the author's handling of the theme that makes it all the more acceptable. Satire and irony are his main tools of mocking the conservative and corrupt elements in society. Ajala's letter of application for work and his school testimonial are written in a stereotyped, stilted official language. So also is the official reply. This contrasts sharply with the simple and conversational English of the author. Language variety is therefore used to contra-distinguish between the progressive and retrogressive elements in society. The author uses dialogue not only as a medium of interaction between characters but also as a ready means of advancing the plot. This is how, for example, Ajala gets to know what his exploiter wants as bribe.

AJALA : [readily] : What is it, sir?
AGBALOWOMERI: Do you know what "kola" is?
AJALA : Yes, sir; Is it not kola nut?
AGBALOWOMERI: [amused] : Ha, that shows that you are a mere boy. Have you parents? What are they doing?
AJALA : My father is a carpenter and my mother is a petty-trader.
AGBALOWOMERI: [seeing that they are humble people who are not likely to put him into trouble] : Good. I don't want to waste your time, or I should have asked you to go back and ask from your parents what "kola" means. To save you this trouble, I'll just tell you in confidence that my "kola" is only five pounds.
AJALA : Five pounds!
AGBALOWOMERI: Five quid, my boy. Nothing goes for nothing, you know. (p. 16).

The speed of exchange in this dialogue is slow and uncertain in consonance with the setting and circumstance. Agbalowomeri, the chief actor in the passage, is an unreliable official who is looking for a way of broaching his dishonest intention to Ajala. He cannot therefore, speak in a simple straightforward language and has to resort to the use of an unorthodox word like "kola". Even when, later in the play, he speaks in moving prose:

> "Please, good Mr. Okoro, have mercy. If you allow this to come out, I shall be ruined. I shall lose my job. I shall be imprisoned. Look at my grey hairs; consider my position and have mercy. How will my people and friends feel when they hear this? How very shameful! How will I dare to show my face outside after this?" (p. 23).

We are not favourably impressed because of the occasion. One is not surprised that the speech fails to achieve its intention. In this play, the author succeeds in making language an essential part of characterization.

The playwright satirizes Durodayo and Babameto for their insiduous attempt to interfere with the dispensation of justice. They assume that their influence on the judge through family ties is great and that this could be used in favour of the arrested Establishment Officer. Each of them deservedly fails to pervert the course of justice and may, in fact, have made things slightly worse for the accused. The judge stands his ground against any corrupt influence. He is impelled by considerations for justice and fair play and his unshakeable belief that all men are equal before the law. By this action, he reminds one of the activities of Titus in Aluko's, *Kinsman and Foreman*, who in the face of great odds stands for the right and offends practically every member of his family.

There is no mistaking where the sympathy of the author lies in this play. He strongly disapproves of the activities of Durodayo and Babameto. There is a touch of irony in the unwholesome attitude to life of these men, who want to destroy a judge, who in various ways is a valuable member of their family. The judge emphasizes this point when he says to Babameto: "Surely, having helped me so much in life, you would not like to ruin me or my reputation?" (p. 34). Again, in the court scene, the author only thinly disguises his support for the prosecution. The case of the defence is presented as weak and untenable. Instead of producing cogent points to buttress his argument the defence counsel attempts to confuse the judge and jury with mere verbiage.

> My lord, members of the Jury, I submit that the whole evidence, such as it is, is tantamount to a complete fabrication, absolutely irresponsible, without foundation and cleverly woven to implicate my client. Where it is not utterly fatuous, it is obviously fictitious. (p. 43).

The court scene is particularly well-handled. It contributes in no small measure to the success of the play, in the way it brings together all the important characters and provides a fitting climax to the work. It affords an opportunity for fierce interaction and theatrical display among members of the two opposing groups. The towering figure of the judge, as an independent arbiter, gives the needed assurance that justice will be done. Justice is openly administered, and the reader leaves the play with the satisfaction that the corrupt will not always escape punishment. This, in the Nigerian situation, makes this work a valuable contribution to Literature at the level of education for which it is intended.

III.

The Incorruptible Judge emphasizes the role of conscience in the administration of justice. This gives the play an edifying content. What makes *Kurunmi* an attractive play is the way it uses the facts of history to dramatise the social realities of the present.[4] Rotimi approaches his work from the angle to tragedy. Kurunmi, the tragic hero, answers to the historical description of "king, judge, general, entertainer, sometimes also executioner".[5] In defence of tradition, he drags his people into a ruinous war, brings untold hardship on his tribe and fights to his doom.

Kurunmi is presented in such a way that his acts and speeches easily attain tragic proportions. His initial moves are utterly convincing. As Are-Ona-Kakanfo he cannot allow tradition to be flouted with impunity. "The day a people lose their tradition is the day their death begins," (p. 16) Kurunmi says in justification for his preparation for war. He is at great pains to emphasize that his hatred for Adelu and his supporters does not stem from any personal consideration but from his obligation to uphold tradition which, to him, is crucial to group survival.

My people, we too have tradition,
This is what makes us men.

---

[4] Ola Rotimi, *Kurunmi* (London: O.U.P., 1971). All page references are to the 1974 edition of the book.

[5] J. F. Ade Ajayi (with R. Smith), *Yoruba Warfare in the Nineteenth Century* (London: C.U.P., 1964), p. 67.

> This is what makes us ... people, distinct from mud.
> Why, the pride of bees is in the honeycomb.
> The pride of the weaver-bird
> shows in the skilful design of its nest.
> And where stands the pride of the monkey?
> Is it not in his knowledge of the secrets on treetops?
> The pride of man, my people,
> is in his tradition (pp. 15–16).

An important achievement of the work is the way the playwright brings before the reader the seriousness of the whole situation. We are made to see a lot of the preparation for war on both sides. The occasional disagreements within the two warring camps of Ijaiye and Ibadan are realistic in the circumstance. Rotimi succeeds in invoking a gloo.ny atmosphere of war in which each side uses every kind of ruthless device, traditional or modern, to wipe out the other. It is not a fight between men only; the gods too play their part with equal acrimony. But the psychological climate has to be created by man for the ancestral gods to intervene in his favour. This is what Areagoro tries to achieve for Ijaiye in the following passage.

> Ogun ... lord of battle it is to you we call,
> and before you we stand.
> It is today one sees,
> the eyes do not see tomorrow.
> Today your children of Ijaiye need your help.
> Today we of Ijaiye are hungry for the disgrace of Ibadan.
> Help us feed on them,
> help us feed on Ibadan.
> There is no god like the throat, it takes sacrifice daily.
> Help us to feed on the destruction of Ibadan.
> This we ask. (p. 60).

Rotimi exercises great economy of words in reporting the war. Each encounter between the warring factions carries the action of the play forward by, at least, one step. Nor does he attempt to record all encounters. Instead, he cleverly uses the diary of Rev. and Mrs. Mann in Act 3, Scenes 5 and 9 to fill in the necessary detail. In this way, he excludes material which may easily become boring. Rotimi has been rightly commended for his technique.

Altogether, Rotimi has been careful not to divert attention from the main concern of the play. The series of battles that take place in Act Three are all important as aspects of the historical event, but the playwright's intention is not to recount the facts of history. Rather, he is interested in the study of man caught up in a particular situation. The battles are important because they help to focus attention on Kurunmi's changing fortunes before the final blow that spells his doom.[6]

This "final blow" comes with the defeat of Kurunmi's army and his eventual downfall.

Rotimi shows versatility not only in his choice of material but also in his use of language. This has helped to make *Kurunmi*, a memorable theatrical experience. His debt to Yoruba oral tradition is obvious from the way he freely juxtaposes in this play tragic and comic elements, a device which he may have derived from the Yoruba sense of humour. When, for example, there is an offer of war from Oyo, Kurunmi pours scorn on his opponents and rejoices at the impending opportunity to humiliate them. Ironically, it is Kurunmi that is ultimately destroyed.

Consider also instances when language is used to provoke laughter and provide comic interlude. Usually it is Kurunmi, who shows contempt for his enemies.

> The frog is kicked — kpa!
> it flattens
> y-a-k-a-t-a!
> on its back.
> We shall all die
> "gbere"
> We shall all die
> "gbere"
> we shall — (pp. 27–28).

The words "kpa", "y-a-k-a-t-a" and "gbere" are onomatopoeic. They help to underline Kurunmi's fatal miscalculations and accentuate the tragic action.

---

[6] Akanji Nasiru, "Ola Rotimi's Search for a Technique" in Kolawole Ogungbesan, ed. *New West African Literature* (London: Heinemann, 1979), pp. 26–27.

There is a touch of irony in the intervention by the whites whether as missionaries, chroniclers or military personnel. They are the only people who exert great pressure to prevent war between Ijaiye and Ibadan. Once the war starts, they try to bring it to a quick end. Rev. & Mrs. Mann follow in detail the fortunes of the war and help to set up a relief operation. Their war records are extremely helpful because they provide an insight into the various events. In a war ostensibly fought to defend indigenous culture and a traditional way of life, why does the only persistent effort to mediate come from foreigners? If this attempt is a genuine one, why does it fail? If the attempt is considered irrelevant, why is so much space devoted to it? The play provides only a partial answer. The three symbols of the tragic play are the war, River Ose and a determined attempt to mediate which fails. If the drift towards tragedy must be complete, then the whites must not only fail in their mediation attempt, but must be presented as incapable of success. This may be Rotimi's intention. For, despite the few comic scenes, *Kurunmi* is conceived as a tragic creation which conforms in many respects with the playwright's conception of the role of the theatre.

> Theatre is not a place where you go just to entertain an array of well-seated businessmen. I see theatre as a force towards the examination of the collective society; the machinery for the awakening of our collective consciousness and perhaps so, as a means towards planning the values — political and social.[7]

IV.

Soyinka's view of the theatre is no less serious. He uses it to dramatize traditional and religious customs and practices in order to highlight their significance, as we find in *The Strong Breed*.[8] The play is constructed around the idea of a scapegoat, who sacrifices

---

[7] Ola Rotimi in Artist's Show Case, a serialised television programme, screened in Lagos on 8 September, 1980 and reported in Reviews by Taju Yusuff in *Daily Times*, 18 September, 1980, p. 17.

[8] Wole Soyinka, *The Strong Breed* (London: C.U.P., 1964) in *Collected Plays 1* (London: C.U.P., 1973). All page references are to this edition.

his life for the happiness of his people. Most of the time there is sin to be expiated, and there is the need for a "carrier" who, ordinarily, should be willing and proud to carry the burden for the community as a whole. Soyinka appears to approve of the religious idea of cleansing. But he also emphasizes the need for adequate spiritual preparation and moral unrightness on the part of the people if the sacrifice made by the carrier is to achieve its sacramental intention.

The "carrier" motif is exploited at three levels, with each level acting as a necessary stage for the next. At an elementary level, a girl who owns a personal "carrier", as it were, drags the effigy around town. While Eman and Sunma argue about the propriety of their leaving the village, the girl asks Ifada to help her beat the "carrier" so that she may soon get well. She has no illusions about the implications of her request and reminds Ifada that she is acting in her own interest.

> But just because you are helping me, don't think it is going to cure you. I am the one who will get well at midnight, do you understand? It is my carrier and it is for me alone. (p. 120)

This shows the seriousness with which the whole idea is taken even at this level.

Ifada's involvement with the girl prepares him for his more important role at the next stage. Ifada is the cause of a violent disagreement between Eman, his friend, and Sunma, who shows very little liking for the idiot. Sunma's dislike for Ifada is not unconnected with the way Eman treats her, as she confesses in this passage:

> Ifada can rouse your pity. And yet if anything, I need more kindness from you. Every time my weakness betrays me, you close your mind against me ...Eman ... Eman ... (p. 118).

Sunma knows that unless Ifada proves acceptable, Eman will almost certainly be picked upon as the scapegoat for the year. We, therefore, have the ironical situation in which Eman, a stranger, who needs to run away for his life insists on remaining in the village throughout the festival period while Sunma, a native of the village, is the one most anxious to leave.

The tragic role of Eman as a "carrier" is the central preoccupation of the play, and to this Soyinka devotes his enormous talent as a dramatist. Initially, Eman is an unwilling carrier. He does not accept his role until he sees his father offering service at a high and respectable level, the most convincing level of performance provided by the play. The old man is getting ready to carry the sins of the villagers for the last time, a duty which Eman ought to have taken over from his father. Eman appears as the old man is about to carry the symbolic dwarf boat, and he is reminded of his duty to the villagers.

> Ours is a strong breed my son. It is only a strong breed that
> can take this boat to the river year after year and wax stronger
> on it. I have taken down each year's evils for over twenty
> years. I hoped you would follow me. (p. 133).

This moment of recognition when Eman is brought face to face with the demanding nature of his moral responsibility to his people is, in a sense, the climax of the play. After a short period of confusion and indecision, he inflexibly resolves to accept his role as a carrier and works with indefatigable energy to fulfil his obligation to his people.

Soyinka adopts a number of skilful dramatic devices in this play to impart a sense of tragic inevitability. The play is set for the eve of the new year, in an atmosphere full of tension and great expectations. The whole village is agog with activities in preparation for the festival. It is against this background that the playwright introduces the melodrama of the unwilling carrier who, in normal circumstances, ought to have been stoned to submission. With the judicious use, as necessary, of pre-dramatic material, flashbacks, pantomine, play within a play, Soyinka gives the reader all the information he requires to understand the tragic circumstances of the play. The reader soon realises the extent to which traditional values need to be reappraised in order for them to accommodate the social realities of the present. The conservative elements in society, in their rigidity, have overplayed their hand and overreached themselves in the process. They end up disillusioned. They have done great damage to tradition in the way they have created doubt in the minds of the people about the relevance of certain aspects of indigenous culture.

JAGUNA : I am sick to the heart of the cowardice, I have seen tonight.
OROGE : That is the nature of men.
JAGUNA : Then it is a sorry world to live in. We did it for them. It was all for their own common good. What did it benefit me whether the man lived or died. But did you see them? One and all they looked up at the man and words died in their throats.
OROGE : It was no common sight.
JAGUNA : Women could not have behaved so shamefully. One by one they crept off like sick dogs. Not one could raise a course.
OROGE : It was not only him they fled. Do you see how unattended we are? (p. 146)

Soyinka's message is clear. He does not invite the reader to deride tradition as the end of the play tends to suggest. He, however, emphasizes the need for modification and change, when necessary. The practice of the carrier is a noble one. If there is sin, there must be a way to expiate it. The idea of the strong breed is an acceptable one. The carrier must be willing, and his practice must not be seen to be in the way of progress. These ideas have been succinctly summarized by Gerald Moore.

> His (Soyinka's) rejection of such characters as the gross Kadiye and the hateful Jaguna does not, as some critics have supposed, amount to a rejection of traditional religious ideas. On the contrary, it is the best of these ideas, together with the ritual and mythology which embody them, that have provided his richest store of metaphor and dramatic symbol; but they call out for reinterpretation in terms of ever-changing values and conditions.[9]

V.

In this paper, an attempt has been made to assess three plays for

---

[9] Gerald Moore, *Wole Soyinka* (London: Evans, 1971), p. 56.

their relevance to the educational process. The plays are written for different levels of education by playwrights of differing capabilities and recognition. Each play has a clear message: *The Incorruptible Judge*, upholds the principle of public morality and accountability; *Kurunmi*, stresses the disaster which results from any attempt to toy with tradition while *The Strong Breed*, emphasizes the need to change or modify traditional ideas and practices whenever circumstances demand this. At the practical level each play is easy to act because of the help given by way of detailed stage directions. In content, language and as a dramatic piece each play could be a valuable aid to education.

An important aim of education is to make the learner develop a realistic attitude to life. For such an aim to be achieved, the school curriculum should provide the necessary incentive for him to apply any knowledge gained to the facts of life. The use of drama develops the learner's imagination, opens for him new horizons and opportunities, gives him creative insights and reinforces his sense of value for things of great cultural and spiritual worth. This results in effective learning.

The goals of Literature is to help project in an imaginative manner the condition of man in society and help the reader become a very useful member of that society. Literature, therefore, cannot be conceived of only in terms of facts and figures. It is the

> Recorded experience of mankind which reflects with truth and comments with illumination upon the life of today and yesterday, the life of the body and the mind, in prose, in verse and in dramatic form.[10]

For work in any literary form to be fully appreciated in the classroom situation, it needs the totality of response which only a well constructed play, produced with maximum class participation, can provide.

---

[10] A. E. Smith, *English in the Modern School*, (London: Methuen & Co., 1959), p. 136.

CHAPTER 9
THE WOMEN NOVELISTS OF WEST AFRICA*

I.

The woman novelist in West Africa works under many literary and social disabilities. She may be academically disadvantaged and may lack the clear artistic vision which results in great works of art. She is almost certainly a late-comer in the field and usually tries, for the most part unsuccessfully, to imitate her male counterpart. In a society dominated by men, she suffers from various kinds of restrictions and limitations which tend to affect adversely the quality of her literary output. If she has not had the opportunity to travel wide, mix freely with different social groups — male and female — and, with others, experience the joys and concerns of her community, she seems hardly well-equipped to produce a successful illusion of life in her novels.

There are many women writers in West Africa. But only a few of them have been able to produce the sustained effort which is required to write a full-length novel. In this paper, three novelists will be considered in some detail — Flora Nwapa, Adaora Ulasi and Ama Ata. It will be shown that the works of Flora Nwapa tend to be superficial and limited in scope, that Miss Ulasi does not always display creative intelligence. On the other hand, Ms. Aidoo rises above many of these limitations in her only novel to produce a genuine work of art. Because she realises fully the African background she achieves universality and thus portrays adequately the condition of man in society. Her work succeeds mainly because of her new and exciting method of communication.

II.

Flora Nwapa's interest in *Efuru* is largely sociological. The author's main purpose seems to be to instruct people in Igbo way

---

*First published in *West African Studies in Modern Language Teaching and Research*, National Language Center, Federal Ministry of Education, Lagos, 1981, pp. 199–211.

of life, especially as it relates to village life, marriage, marital life, child-bearing and matrimonial relationships. Her main preoccupation is with childlessness and the disastrous effect this has on marital life in a rural African setting. This is a powerful subject which, if imaginatively handled, can result in great literature. But because of the literal manner in which the novelist narrates her story, any dramatic impact which it might have had is almost completely lost.

Even when very occasionally, Flora Nwapa attains moments of great tension, her power of execution fails her. A case in point is the encounter between Eneberi (Gilbert) and Ajanupu when Efuru is critically ill. Eneberi accuses Efuru of adultery to which she must confess to get well. Ajanupu is naturally outraged by this accusation and rains curses on Eneberi.

> Eneberi, nothing will be good for you henceforth Eneberi, Ajanupu, the daughter of Uberife Nkemjika of Umuosuma village, says that from henceforth nothing good will come your way. Our ancestors will punish you. Our Uhamiri will drown you in the Great River. From henceforth evil will continue to visit you.[1]

Eneberi loses his temper, gives Ajanupu a slap and pushes her down. A fight takes place between the two and Ajanupu breaks Eneberi's head with a mortar pestle. That is all we are told about this ugly incident which might have been used to establish Efuru's innocence and expose Eneberi's credulity. There is definitely an artistic failure here. Given the usual friendly relationship between Ajanupu and Eneberi, this incident should have been regarded as outrageous and ought to have been accorded the dramatic importance it deserves. Again, nothing in Ajanupu's character can lead the reader to believe that she will allow Eneberi to go without further punishment for his rash decision and behaviour.

Flora Nwapa does only a little better with characterisation. No male character develops. Adizua and Gilbert, who are variously assigned major roles as the husbands of Efuru at different times do not show any development in character commensurate with their individual responsibility. True, the courtship between Gilbert and

---

[1] Flora Nwapa, *Efuru* (London, 1966), p. 275.

Efuru is well-handled, and the author appears more successful with her female characters. Ogea grows from the weak position of a domestic to play important roles in family affairs. Ajanupu is presented as a strong character throughout and is Efuru's constant support in times of distress. The author's intimate knowledge of domestic matters, the relationship between Efuru and Ajanupu, the roles of Ogea and other female characters, Efuru's upbringing of children and disposition to her two husbands — all help to make this essentially a woman's novel. The world of the novel is dominated by woman and feminine practices.

> Efuru gave Ogonim a hot bath and put mentholatum in her anus. She then rubbed kernel oil all over her body putting it in every opening of the body. She tried to breastfeed her, but she refused it. Efuru put her on her back and in no time she was asleep. She brought her out again and put her on the bed. "Now stay with her Ogea, while I go to Ajanupu."
>
> Efuru walked as fast as she could, occasionally breaking into a run. Ajanupu was in. 'My daughter is ill,' she told Ajanupu before she sat down. 'She has a fever and she has lost her appetite. I have rubbed her with kernel oil.'[2]

Perhaps only a woman, who is herself a mother can write such an intimate piece on mother care. Such details occasionally, impart realism to Flora Nwapa's characterization.

However, the presentation of Efuru as an elegant, prosperous, infinitely patient, almost perfect village woman greatly respected by all, presents difficulties. The work abounds with examples of her goodness, and she is endowed with superhuman qualities: Gilbert spends the night out several times without notice and comes in the following morning without a word of rebuke (or complaint) from Efuru; Efuru takes care of the mother of Adizua who cruelly deserts her, decides on her own to get a new wife for Gilbert, her husband, and accepts her husband's boy by another woman even though Gilbert does not give her any previous warning about the boy.

Efuru is too good to be a convincing character. She reminds one of Ihuoma in *The Concubine*, where Amadi attempts a beautiful,

---

[2] *Ibid.*, p. 77.

almost perfect character.[3] Amadi's character achieves credibility because of the author's method of delineation. The reader, through the author's use of appropriate details, comes to regard Ihuoma as a rational human being and accept the nature of her connection with the Gea-King. "The creation of perfect or near-perfect characters," says Eustace Palmer, "is a task of considerable difficulty, which Amadi has undertaken with great success. Ihuoma's goodness, politeness, courage, chastity, modesty, good sense, selflessness and beauty, are not only commented on but demonstrated."[4] Flora Nwapa gives no reason for Efuru's goodness and does not offer enough detail to make her role in the novel acceptable.

III.

Idu is the same kind of novel as *Efuru*. Both novels thrive on assumed childlessness, and there are cross references from one to the other. There is, for example, a reference to Efuru's house in *Idu*. Also, the woman of the Lake appears in both novels and in each case she is given the same kind of role, an omnipresent god who directs the affairs of man. She is endowed with enormous mysterious supernatural power. She alone could have been responsible for the death of Efuru and Idu, or rather these deaths could not have taken place without her permission or collaboration.

However, Flora Nwapa shows some signs of artistic maturity in *Idu*. Although there is still the use of material in a sociological way, dialogue is freer, and the novelist displays an incisive knowledge of the content and tenor of village gossip. Signs of slight improvement are clear right from the beginning of the book:

> "You had a maid, what happened to her?"
> "She has gone. Her people came for her, one day, and she went with them; I did not even know she took all the dresses I made for her, and left my youngest daughter crying."
> "That is bad. Who are her people?"
> "She is from Esu," Nwasobi replied. "They are like that. You cannot rely on them. Look, there's Idu. Idu, our Idu, are you well?"

---

[3] Elechi Amadi, *The Concubine* (London, 1966).
[4] Eustace Palmer, *An Introduction to the African Novel* (London, 1972), p. 120.

The Women Novelists of West Africa 141

"I am very well," replied Idu. "I have come to fetch some water. My husband is not very well today."
"What's wrong with him?" Nwasobi asked.
"He had a headache yesterday, so..."[5]

Here dialogue is free and relevant. It is used not only to introduce some of the principal characters of the book; it also touches on a theme which is central to the action of the novel.

In this book, the author seizes every opportunity to dramatise the fears, beliefs and doubts of the people. Occasionally, she attains heights of dramatic tension, usually achieved through the exploitation of the people's rural simplicity. The appearance of an eclipse is a case in point. The novelist uses this incident to expose the people's ignorance of a natural phenomenon. They are thrown into a panic and cease all normal activities. They are shown to be men and women of very limited mental horizon:

> It was the end of the world. Who among the people could claim that he had ever seen the night in the middle of the day? How could night occur twice in one day? It was unheard of. The world was full of evil men, and God was manifesting. His works among men of the earth. The darkness had come so suddenly, without a warning. To the Christians it was the coming of Christ. He was to come like a thief in the night, unheralded.[6]

Even a greater confusion arises when Ijoma is presumed lost. The whole community is involved in the search and the novelist uses this occasion to bring about communal solidarity. Idu's pathetic cry: "My Ijoma, where is my Ijoma, where is my only son? Where is my only child? Has he drowned? Maybe he went to the lake and was drowned. In that case we shall see his body floating tomorrow morning."[7] gives the signal for an intensive search in which practically every villager takes part. The genuineness of the people's distress and the thorough and energetic manner in which they show their concern attest to their love and respect for Idu. The author's

---

[5] Flora Nwapa, *Idu* (London, 1970), p. 1.
[6] *Ibid.*, p. 82.
[7] *Ibid.*, p. 189.

achievement here is obvious in the way she successfully mobilises the people for a humanitarian purpose.

This notwithstanding, *Idu* cannot be said to be on the whole a successful novel. Facts are still presented, for the most part, in a literal fashion. Inanities abound in the conversation of villagers. Many of the characters do not have a relevant purpose in the novel. Only Idu and Anamadi show any signs of physical or mental development. Nwasobi is a weak substitute for Ajanupa of *Efuru*. One therefore, cannot but agree with Yinka Shoga's opinion of these novels:

> The novels of Flora Nwapa have a diffused quality that prevents them having a very strong impart. The lot of woman is developed in a personal rather than a social term. The limitations imposed on the woman by the society is accepted by the character as well as the novelist. Consequently the novels lack that universal importance, that amplitude of reference which comes from the clash of human aspirations with destiny. So, the untimely death at the end may be pathetic, even shocking but definitely not tragic.[8]

IV.

The artistic limitations of the first two novels of Adaora Ulasi are even more crippling than those which have been identified in Flora Nwapa's works.[9] With Miss Ulasi, there appears to be a certain misconception of the functions of a work of art and a demonstrated inability to create successfully an illusion of life in her novels. The result is a constant breakdown in communication between groups in the novels and between the artist and her audience.

The works take the form of detective novels. They seem only pseudo-satirical because the medium of communication makes it difficult for the author to realise her intentions. Miss Ulasi's chosen medium is pidgin English, and this most characters speak.

---

[8] Yinka Shoga, "Women Writers and African Literature," *Afriscope*, Vol. 3, No. 10, (October, 1973), p. 44.
[9] Miss Ulasi's first two novels are:
1. *Many Thing You No Understand* (London, 1970).
2. *Many Thing Begin for Change* (London, 1971).

The Women Novelists of West Africa 143

"My countrymen, Okafor come this evening-time with disturbing news. We no talk about this bad news too much. We decide for you all to hear this news with your own ears and then we trash the matter out together."

Having spoken, Chukwuka turned to Okafor, for him to enlighten the newcomers.

Okafor began: "You know when Chief Obezie die, we needed something, according to native law and custom and for the sake of him dignity, to bury him with. And so, you decide that it fall on Chukwuka here, and myself, to do that necessary thing."

There were murmurs of assent.

"So," Okafor went on, "we did the thing you ask us to do until nearly the finish. The last man we catch from the village of Ntu give much trouble. His small brother come out and he see us."[10]

Pidgin English is used here in the wrong situation. Igbo elders in conclave are not likely to address one another in Pidgin on a matter which touches on their survival as a people. The author's medium does not reflect the importance of the developing situation. It is unconvincing and destroys the basis of true characterization.[11]

The breakdown in communication between the colonial authority and the people is achieved in several ways. Apart from any differences in language and orientation, each group is given a different role to play. There is an insidious attempt to capitalise on the mutual suspicion which, usually, exists between a colonising power and the people, who feel so heavily oppressed. So, although MacIntosh hands down fair judgements in the court cases in *Many Thing You No Understand*, the people receive the verdicts with misgivings. The kidnapping of the District Officer in Miss Ulasi's second novel is the most concrete external manifastation of the deep-seated resentment which the people have against the Administration. The author dramatises successfully the disenchantment of the people. She might have been more effective if she did not write in Pidgin English — a medium with which she is apparently not familiar.

---

[10] *Many Thing You No Understand*, pp. 78–79.
[11] For further discussion of this aspect of Miss Ulasi's works, see relevant sections of Chapter Two in Oladele Taiwo, *Culture and the Nigerian Novel* (London, 1976).

V.

Miss Ulasi's third novel, *The Night Harry Died*, is different from the first two in many respects.[12] It is set against the background of Southern U.S.A., unlike the others, whose setting is in Eastern Nigeria. The medium of expression in the third novel is standard English even though the author shows fascination for the habits of speech of the people she writes about. No more do we have the ruinous effect of Pidgin English on this work as in the previous ones. It might well be that Miss Ulasi, herself, had become conscious of the fact that she was not doing well with Pidgin and had decided to drop it in favour of a medium she became thoroughly familiar with during her long stay in the United States.

In *The Night Harry Died*, Miss Ulasi has an important theme and a consistent imaginative scheme. She appears to have submitted both this time, much more than she has ever done, to the process of creative digestion. The result is a story which is not only interesting in itself, but reveals the author's creative inventiveness and artistic intelligence. Harry Collier is presumed dead, but appears bemused at his own funeral. The novelist shows great powers of description in the way she records the consternation of the people and the chaos which follows:

> The funeral party turned and froze. For there, standing and watching his own funeral procession was Harry Collier! There was a stampede, as the mourners thought they were seeing a ghost. Helm's appeal for calm and common sense went unheeded.
> "Man alive!" shouted Isaiah, the undertaker, and sank into the nearest pew, while Wade, his assistant, loosened Isaiah's collar to give him some air. The undertaker rubbed his eyes, raised his head and took another horrified look.
> But just as suddenly as he'd appeared, Harry vanished. "After him!" shouted the sheriff. Edna clutched the undertaker by the coat and demanded: "Who's in the coffin, then, Mr. Watson? What have you done with Harry?"[13]

---

[12] Adaora Ulasi, *The Night Harry Died* (Lagos, 1974).
[13] *The Night Harry Died*, p. 29.

A serious situation develops and the mystery of Harry's death is not unravelled until a court action is instituted and the principal characters are made to confess their various roles. Part of the novelist's success in this work derives from the fact that, in the midst of this confusion and uncertainty, all is not death, all is not gloom. Through the use of humorous situations and sayings she throws some light on the mystifying episode and, in a way, lightens the burden of the people. If the situation is too serious for anyone to laugh heartily, it is at least helpful to have occasional reliefs:

> There was the firm of Adams and Adams near the church. Harry's father told him that the first Adams built the law firm near the church because it was handy to nip and cleanse one's soul each time one had finished a property deal.[14]

The court scene provides the climax to this work and it is important in the way it gives the clue to the mystery which engulfs the town for so long. Nothing shows more clearly the improvement in the author's artistic ability than the way she handles this court scene. Compared with the court scene at the beginning of *Many Thing You No Understand*, we see here a relevant experience fully integrated into the structure of the novel. No more do we have the needless tomfoolery in court and the purposeless ridiculing of court proceedings which are characteristic features of the previous attempt. Proceedings are now conducted according to the rules and with great adroitness.

> "Now, I don't want any noise around her," shouted the judge, glaring at the packed court through blood-shot eyes. He gave Lacey the signal to continue.
> "You say you stayed with Mrs. Collier, Sam. For how long would that be?"
> "Reckon about a couple of months, sir."
> "And what happened between you two all that time you stayed with her?"
> "I object, your honour," cried Adams. "It is a pretty insinuating question that the sheriff's trying to ask there."
> "Objection sustained," the judge said.

---

[14] *Ibid.*, p. 24.

"When you lived with Mrs. Collier, did you help around the shack?" asked the sheriff, and Sam replied in the affirmative.
"Reckon we all here know there's nothing much to do around a shack like that. In what way did you help Edna Collier?"
"Objection, your honour," Adams interjected again.
Judge Albert looked at the Lawyer, a little annoyed. "Well, Mr. Adams. I don't see you've much to object about."[15]

The novelist has undoubtedly matured and can now present a complex situation in simple, if formal, English. But it seems ironical that the author has been more successful with the work based on the U.S.A., than with those based on Nigeria which she should know more intimately. A narrow view of what constitutes African Literature may exclude *The Night Harry Died*, even though it is written by an African and accept the first two novels on the grounds that they are African in content, authorship, sympathy, conception and execution. It would be a pity to exclude a successful work of art on the grounds of content. Any categorisation should be on the grounds of relevance and level of performance.

VI.

Many of the problems of communication we have encountered with other female novelists do not arise with Ama Ata Aidoo. *Our Sister Killjoy* — a novel in four chapters — is a new thing in structure and provides a fresh approach to fiction-writing in West Africa.[16] One of the highlights of the novel is that it is written in a combination of poetry and prose. The poetry runs so naturally into narrative or dialogue that one does not always know whether to take it at face value or try to read between the lines. This does not always make the work of interpretation easy. The novel derives its complexity from the fact that, although in a few cases the literal meaning would do, for the most part a secondary meaning must be sought to get the full import of the novelist's message:

---

[15] *Ibid.*, p. 99.
[16] Ama Ata Aidoo, *Our Sister Killjoy* (London, 1977).

"Mary... Mary... Mary. Did you say in school zey call you Mary?"
"Yes."
"Like me?"
"Yes."
"Vai?"
"I come from a Christian family. It is the name they gave me when they baptised me. It is also good for school and work and being a lady."
"Mary, Mary... and you an African?"
"Yes."
"But that is a German name!" said Marija.

. . . .

But my brother
They got
Far
Enough
Teaching among other things,
Many other things
That
For a child to grow up
To be a
Heaven-worthy individual
He had
to have
above all, a
Christian name.

And what shall it profit a native that
He should have
systems to give
A boy
A girl
Two
Three names or
More.[17]

A passage like this introduces us, in style and content, to Ms.

---

[17] *Our Sister Killjoy*, pp. 24–26.

Aidoo's complex art. Here dialogue merges easily into narrative and poetry with no strict demarcation between the various forms. The passage gives us some insight into the relationship between Sissie and Marija, a relationship which is central to the concern of the book. The differences and similarities between Africa and Germany are alluded to. As in other parts of the novel, the missionaries are rebuked for some of their activities. A case in point is their imposition of European names on Africans and the obnoxious belief that these names are instrinsically superior to African names.

Ms. Aidoo takes Africa, especially West Africa, as her point of departure, uses Sissie, her main character, to reflect on various things or react with different groups. She is the touchstone against which every person, institution or event is judged. The novelist's purpose is clearly satirical and nobody is spared — the West Africans who live abroad because foreign countries are more comfortable than home, the "academic-pseudo-intellectual", students, politicians. This writer comes down very heavily upon the privileged class. The rulers are considered incompetent and selfish:

> From all around the Third World
> You hear the same story
> Rulers
> Asleep to all things at
> All times —
> Conscious only of
> Riches, which they gather in a
> Coma —
> Intravenously —[18]

and the academics are satirized for their ineffectiveness and vanity:

> Dear Lord
> So what can we do about
> Children not going to school
> When
> Our representatives and interpreters
> The low-achieving academics

---

[18] *Ibid.*, p. 34.

In low profile politics
Have the time of their lives
Grinning at cocktail parties and around
Conference tables?
At least, they made it, didn't they?

No,
Man does not live by
Garri or ugali alone —
Therefore
We do not complain about
Expensive trips to
Foreign 'Varsities where
Honorary doctorate degrees
Come with afternoon teas and
Mouldy Saxon cakes from
Mouldier Saxon dames...[19]

The novelist shows an amazing control of language and situation and proves that a novel can do away almost entirely with sociological material. This author also proves through the efficient manner the material in this work is handled that, however frequently the locale of the events of a novel may change, that needn't affect its unity as a work of art. All that is required is an overriding passion which, in this case, seems to be the total emancipation of Africa. What we have now is no more than "a dance of the masquerades called Independence."[20] The novelist wants this to be translated to true independence — political, social and economic. She hopes for a situation in which Africans will be able to uphold their ancestral values and yet feel equal to any other race in the world. This is the noble wish, the impelling force which has led Ms. Aidoo to her achievement in this novel. The motivating force in her case is undoubtedly the determination to leave Africa a much better place than she met it.

---

[19] *Ibid.*, pp. 57–58.
[20] *Ibid.*, p. 95.

VII.

West Africa is experiencing a cultural rebirth in which the women are playing an active part. This paper has considered the role of the better known women novelists and found that some of them are not as effective as they may have been. The main weaknesses have been in the areas of language, characterization, scope of work, among others. It is not altogether surprising that because of the sustained effort required for fiction writing women have not been as successful with the novel as they have been with, for example, poetry, drama or even the short story.

One wonders whether the problem here is totally unconnected with the social role expected of women in society. As Yinka Shoga explains:

> If society expects a woman to defer to male views and suppress her own, and creation is supremely an act of will directed by a vivid and unique point of view, the woman writer is at a disadvantage. The social situation militates against her being able to create memorable works of art.[21]

This probably explains why there has been no major novel by a female West African writer and why the most memorable female characters in the West African novel have been created by men. Women novelists, for some inexplicable reasons, appear shy to make female characters the central figures of their novels.

One hopes the novel by Ama Ata Aidoo, points the way to the future. As African Literature moves further away from cultural conflicts and ancestral shrines and comes to grip more and more with the dilemmas of the present, as more female writers liberate themselves from the literary prejudices of the past and feel the urge to contribute more meaningfully to the issues of the day, the present limitations on women novelists will become a thing of the past. A useful beginning can be made by the women writers attempting to benefit from their male counterparts in the areas of language, different levels of speech, realistic characterisation and depth of material. It is only then that they can start to establish

---

[21] Yinka Shoga, *op. cit.*, p. 44.

a tradition which other women novelists will build upon. What is required for now is a bold step forward in fiction-writing by women writers in West Africa.

CHAPTER 10
LANGUAGE AND THEME IN THREE AFRICAN NOVELS*

I.

Modern African fiction in English has passed through many phases and has been presented from varying viewpoints. The literary standpoint of a writer imposes its own kind of responsibility. Some novelists are mainly preoccupied with the relationship between the past and the present, especially the significance which the past has for the present. They, like Achebe, feel that the writer's duty is "to explore in depth the human condition. In Africa, he cannot perform this task unless he has a proper sense of history."[1] Other writers, like Soyinka and Ngugi wa Thiong'o, believe that while a sense of history may be useful, the social criticism of contemporary experience should be given utmost priority. The artist should provide a clear vision of a future society.

> It is about time that the African writer stopped being a mere chronicler and understood also that part of his essential purpose is to write with a clear vision ... he must at least begin by exposing the future in a clear and truthful exposition of the present.[2]

Such criticisms may become bitter when they relate to cases of oppression and complete or partial denial of rights. As is the case in Southern Africa, a novelist may find himself living with the iniquitous system of apartheid. What he sees and reads everyday compels his attention and affects his sensibility. He is moved to great emotional heights by the common sufferings of humanity. He writes novels which not only condemn but also show his active

---

*First published in *The Literary Half-Yearly* (Mysore, India) XXII/I, January 1981, pp. 29—45.
[1] Chinua Achebe, "The Role of the Writer in a New Nation". Douglas Killam, ed., *African Writers on African Writing* (London: Heinemann, 1973), p. 8.
[2] Wole Soyinka "The Writer in a Modern African State," in Per Wastberg, ed., *The Writer in Modern Africa* (Uppsala: Scandinavian Institute of African Studies, 1968), p. 58.

support for the creative struggle of the masses. It is essential for success in this kind of writing that the main characters in a work of fiction are involved in the dialectics of struggle. For, as Ngugi wa Thiong'o has said:

> It is not enough for the African artist, standing aloof, to view society and highlight its weaknesses. He must try to go beyond this, to seek out the sources, the causes and the trends of a revolutionary struggle which has already destroyed the traditional power-map drawn up by the colonialist nations.[3]

What meaning we attach to a novel depends largely on how we conceive of it as a work of art. If the novel works only at the literal level as in *Efuru* and *Wand of Noble Wood*, for example, then it is of very little literary worth. But where it works at both the literal and symbolic levels as, for instance, in *The Beautiful Ones Are Not Yet Born* and *A Grain of Wheat*, the work is more aesthetically satisfying. Often it is language, theme and presentation which make the difference. For example, one cannot hope to derive much meaning from *The Beautiful Ones* without paying necessary attention to the use of symbolism. Nor can any thoughtful literary comment on *The Palm-Wine Drinkard* fail to emphasize the symbolic importance of the Drinkard's journey to the land of the dead — that it is a journey made to achieve rebirth and spiritual growth.

These considerations lead us to think that language and theme are important in the determination of meaning in any work of fiction. Language is not necessarily conceived in a sense of that kind of unique experimentation one finds, for example, in Tutuola and Okara, but as a medium through which a novelist presents those aspects of life he has selected for treatment. For, as has been said elsewhere:

> A writer's language is a mirror held up to his personality and his particular circumstances. It is through the use of language that he reflects his individual awareness of a given situation. The detailed study of language leads, almost in-

---

[3] Ngugi wa Thiong'o, Wole Soyinka, T. M. Aluko and the Satiric Voice, in *Homecoming* (London: Heinemann, 1972), pp. 65–6.

evitably, to a consideration of the more fundamental problems of communication.[4]

In this paper, an attempt will be made to show that language and theme are so closely interrelated that one can hardly be separated from the other in a well executed work. The approach adopted is one of close analysis of texts, and the broad aim is to determine how successfully a novelist dramatises in a chosen work the realities and dilemmas of the present. Three works are discussed in detail to show how the theme and language of a writer affect the meaning and reception of his work. The choice of novels is deliberate; they represent different parts of the continent and periods of history in order to show what influence time and place can exert on the theme and language of a novel. Close attention will be given to the resources of language available to each writer and the use he makes of them in the presentation of his material.

II.

The Slave is a parable of a determined human effort that is destined to fail.[5] Olumati (Olu, for short) finds himself, through no fault of his, a slave at the shrine of Amadioha quite early in life. He tries hard to free himself from this bondage. He returns to his people to establish himself and revitalise the family compound which is in ruins. He achieves initial successes, but his attempt to make a name for himself among his people ends in disgrace. He returns to the shrine of Amadioha whence he come.

In this novel, as in *The Concubine* and *The Great Ponds*, Amadi describes a society that is pre-colonial (perhaps pre-historic) and is therefore not disturbed in any way by external influences. Social life is under the superintendence of the gods, who control human destiny and against whose judgements and decisions man is powerless. People live a communal life and believe that the action of an individual member can bring great joy or calamity, as the case may be, on the community as a whole. The protection of the gods is considered so essential that men take every kind of step to ensure

---

[4] Oladele Taiwo, *Culture and the Nigerian Novel* (London: Macmillan, 1976), p. XIV.
[5] Elechi Amadi, *The Slave* (London: Heinemann, 1978). All page references are to this edition.

that no evil spirit comes between them and their gods. That is why, for instance, Olumati takes necessary precautions, with the help of Ajohia, the dibia, to ensure that his new house is well protected against any evil influence.

This is the background against which Amadi writes in, *The Slave*. The story achieves its dramatic impact from the harmony between theme and language which is evident virtually on every page. Language used on each occasion is dictated by the given circumstance, character and setting. The novelist shows himself a master of narrative prose.

> Ali will protect you, my son. Now to the point. When your family scattered, neighbouring families farmed parts of your land after they had waited for years. If this had not been done all your farmlands would have reverted to jungle and farming would have been very difficult thereafter. After so many years it will not be easy for those who have been farming on your family land to let go; but I shall help you when the time comes. Listen well. A newly-bought chicken stands cautiously on one leg to begin with. You should do the same. Do not hope to recover all that is yours in a day or two or even in a year or two. If you rush you will find things very difficult. You should lick hot soup slowly from the sides. (p. 30)

Amadi uses all the resources of his first language to write prose of great distinction. In this passage, he uses all the devices of speech available to an old man talking direct to a young person. The setting is friendly enough. Minikwe tries to help Olumati set himself up after a long period of absence from his ancestral farmland. "Ali will protect you, my son" is the sort of beginning which can make Olumati feel at home, and "Now to the point" is meant to be a businesslike introduction to the main narration which is given in convincing prose. The argument of the passage cannot be faulted; it is, in fact, clinched by two meaningful proverbs. "Listen well" is a rhetorical device to ensure that Olumati does not miss the essence of the old man's message. Hence, it comes just before the proverbs. In the first proverb, Olumati is the "newly bought chicken", who should stand "cautiously on one leg to begin with." In the second, he is advised to "lick hot soup slowly from the sides." The proverbs contain images and idioms deeply rooted in indigenous culture, adequately summarise the substance of the old man's speech and help to drive home his point.

The novel owes most of its success to the interaction among characters and the efficient way this is handled. The novelist creates a number of love entanglements so that in their successful resolution his skill as a writer may be easily appreciated. Enaa, the beautiful girl in mgbede, is the natural centre of attraction. So, Olumati and Wizo, who are friends, and others woo her. Nyeche makes advances to Enaa and Aleru, who are friends, and ends up with Aleru. There are confrontations and conflicts, a natural phenomenon in any community. Whether the occasion is the death of Nyege or the marriage of Aleru, villagers show their sincere affection for one another. This sincerity is often reflected in the dialogue which takes place among villagers. In a situation which allows for some display of emotion, dialogue appears a natural medium for individuals to lay bare their thoughts and a ready means of carrying the story forward, as this encounter between Enaa and Aso shows.

"Enaa".
"Mm".
"I want to marry you."
There was silence
"Mm?"
Enaa paused to think.
"Mm?"
"As you said, your family has made contact with mine."
"That is true."
"You will get an answer through my father."
I know, but two of us should agree secretly first.
It would make things easier."
"I can't give you an answer here and now."
"Why not?"
"I have to think about it."
"When should I expect an answer?"
"Perhaps when I am out of mgbede." (p. 96).

The circumstance and manner of exchange reveals the degree of candour which villagers show to one another. In this passage, a serious matter — a marriage proposal — is approached with caution. "I want to marry you", comes from Aso after considerable thought and Enaa's reply must naturally take some time. Hence, we are told: "There was silence." The period of silence serves two purposes: it gives Enaa an opportunity to think over her reply and assures Aso that whatever reply he gets is not a hasty one, and can therefore serve as a basis for further discussion. Thus, silence is used here, as elsewhere, as a non-verbal mode of communication. After this rather slow start, the speed of exchange becomes fast, and the lovers speak frankly to each other. "I can't give you an answer here and now" is to be expected in a traditional setting on a matter in which parents usually have the last say. The lovers are made to speak in short, simple and lucid sentences which reflect the love and affection they have for each other. This manner of speaking is one of the ways in which the novelist gives us a hint that this proposal may eventually succeed.

The whole story is built around Enaa. Practically every important person in the community has some personal or official business with her. The institution of the mgbede is glorified and presented as an extremely desirable experience for a girl. It is an exercise in chastity and a preparation for the woman's crucial role in society. It is not surprising, therefore, that Enaa is made to play such a significant role. Every important event, pleasant or tragic, derives from her or from the fact that, she is in mgbede. Olumati's disaster is intimately connected with his love for Enaa, which initially he cannot publicly profess. He confesses his problem to his sister.

> "Believe me, Enaa likes you very much."
> "That does not mean she will marry me."
> "I think she will."
> "Has she told you so?"
> "It is a good guess."
> Olumati laughed shortly.
> "I shall ask her anyway."
> "When?"
> "A year from now."
> "That is too long."
> "She is in mgbede and there is no hurry."
> "Besides, that would give me enough time to prepare." (p. 69)

"A year from now" is the author's way of sounding a tragic note. True, Olumati has become an accomplished wrestler during the period. But one tragic event follows another to destroy him socially: the death of his grandmother, Nyege, and his sister, Aleru; the hatred of members of Okani family, and Enaa's consent to marry Wizo, Olumati becomes so dispirited that he neglects Adiba, who loves him very much and has shown it in various ways,

> "Olu, you have to protect yourself."
> "I know."
> "You are in danger."
> "I know."
> "You don't know how malignant members of Okani family are."
> "I know."
> "I thought you said your mother would come to stay with you."
> "She seems to have changed her mind since Aleru died."
> "You need the services of a very powerful dibia."
> "That is true."
> She sighed.
> "May the day break." There was a tremor in her voice.
> "I shall see you off to the main road."
> "No, stop here."
> Olumati moved on but she stopped and barred his way. (p.150).

This is not a pleasant encounter; so the author makes it as brief as possible. He achieves this mainly through the use of short sentences and the rapid exchange of information between the two speakers. Olumati is uncommunicative, and gives for the most part only short replies like 'I know' (repeated three times) and "That is true." "You are in danger", succinctly summarizes his personal circumstances at the moment and may be responsible for his reticence. The whole passage conjures up an atmosphere of gloom and foreboding and helps to emphasize the fact that Olumati needs "the services of a very powerful dibia". The "tremor" in the girl's voice is meant to underscore the hopelessness of the situation in which Olumati finds himself.

Olumati's mental confusion is such that he no longer trusts anybody in the community. He is not touched by Adiba's show of affection. One is moved to pity for a man, who is being made to suffer for the guilt of others. Language is used in this passage as a medium through which the novelist's sympathies are revealed and people's motives and actions are portrayed and evaluated.

III.

Language in, *The Slave* is used as a means of integrating the villager more firmly with his indigenous culture. It has therefore, for the most part, been sober, dignified, unobtrusive and functional.

In *Carcase for Hounds* one is confronted with a situation where the seriousness of the theme is reflected in the narrative intensity and continuity of the prose.[6] Nwangi is involved with the analysis of events of great national importance. What we have in this novel is the presentation of national history in a favourable light. Mau Mau is portrayed as a justifiable resistance movement against white oppression, the only reliable means open to the masses to regain their land and human dignity. Haraka is the embodiment of this hope which the vast majority of the people cherish. However, to the Government, Mau Mau is evil which needs to be urgently uprooted, and Haraka is a monster who must be immediately annihilated. Captain Kingsley, the man who has the ugly business of accomplishing this gigantic task, has a love-hate relationship with Haraka. It is within these conflicts and confrontations that the novelist sets his tragic theme. His overall achievement lies in the way he is able, through his controlled and unpretentious prose style, to bring the events of the novel vividly, as it were, before the eyes of the reader. The high quality of the novelist's prose is evident in a passage like this:

> The water in the ditches had gone down to only a few inches deep. The radio Land-Rover was shoved and tugged out of its grave back to the road. That too headed for Pinewood. The three-tonner presented a more difficult problem. It was heavier and lay at a bad angle. It took some figuring out even before they started the real physical work. Then the driver climbed in and started the engine. It roared hoarsely and the truck lunged forward. Then it slipped and rocked back into the ditch. The soldiers positioned themselves around it and dug their boots into the soft ground. (p. 91).

This passage shows the novelist has an eye for details. It also

---

[6] Meja Nwangi, *Carcase for Hounds* (London: Heinemann, 1974). All page references are to this edition.

introduces the reader to the central concern of the novel — the gruesome encounter between government forces and Mau Mau, especially the personal contributions of Haraka and Kingsley. It is to this theme that the author devotes his best narrative energy. The effectiveness of the novelist's narration derives from his accurate and systematic description of events, especially his use of appropriate words and expressions. In the sentence, "The radio Land-Rover was shoved and tugged out of its grave back to the road", the weight of meaning is aptly placed on "shoved" and "tugged" while the metaphoric use of "grave" brings to the reader's mind, the picture of a Land-Rover "restored to life" after a period of incapacitation. In the same manner, the three-tonner is endowed with human qualities in "It *roared* hoarsely and the truck *lunged* forward..." It is through the use of such linguistic devices that the novelist makes his imaginary world real and attractive.

The novel provides a lot of material on how Mau Mau is organized and the methods adopted by the leaders to secure and retain the sympathy and loyalty of their followers. Mau Mau is confronted with an efficient government force and propaganda machine. There is also the problem of stooges like Simba. Government resources in men and material are enormous, the organization on the ground, almost perfect; yet the task of bringing down the Mau Mau rebellion proves extremely difficult. The novel provides an answer to this mystery — the Mau Mau fighters are very much at home in the jungle which is the arena of war. The picture provided is that of a running battle in which the superior weapons and resources of government forces confer no advantage. A lot of credit is given to Haraka and his men for being able to outwit government forces and continue the struggle in difficult circumstances.

> The flight back to the forest was executed quickly and efficiently, true to the general's reputation. By daybreak, the gang was less than three miles from their bamboo base. At noon they were settled back in their home base and lunch was roasting. (p. 70).

Given the novelist's attempt to portray the Mau Mau movement in a favourable light, it is not surprising that so much attention is devoted to General Haraka. Haraka's character is superbly realised through the detailed descriptions of his activities, his ubiquity, his attractive passages of introspection and, especially, the tragedy of his last days. He is presented as absolutely fearless, a man wholly devoted to a laudable cause, a warrior, who thinks very little of his personal safety or convenience. He is a man of great organizational ability and personal magnificence.

Haraka has all the qualities required of a leader to run an organization like the Mau Mau. His method is necessarily ruthless because of the need to ensure continued support of his fighters and eliminate at any stage those, whose loyalty becomes doubtful. He is imbued with a keen sense of loyalty to the cause and succeeds in transmitting this to his followers. The British soon realise that they cannot hope to defeat Mau Mau without first capturing and destroying Haraka. So, Haraka becomes the object of all their military endeavours. The massive man-hunt set up by the British forces fails of its intention and, as far as they know, Haraka remains triumphant to the end, a symbol of resistance and terror. In the words of Eustace Palmer, Haraka is

> A veritable superman whose mysterious presence dominates the novel. Mwangi evokes a convincing impression of his imposing bulk, his tremendous physical strength and courage, and his mysteriousness. The very mention of his name is enough to make grown men wet their pants, and he easily becomes a legend, the man whom the English troops must get at all costs, dead or alive.[7]

Haraka is human and, in order to present him as a rounded character, other aspects of his life are explored. We find that he is not completely devoid of human emotion. He can break down in times of distress; he can become dejected, especially when immobilized by pain or disease. The novelist uses the loneliness of Haraka's last days to provide several examples of his display of human emotion.

Captain Kingsley as leader of government forces is presented as a bitter opponent of Haraka and Mau Mau. The captain is wholly devoted to duty and prosecutes the war to a bitter end. But his best effort does not seem to satisfy the Emergency Council. He is constantly harassed by telephone calls from Brigadier Thomas, who underestimates the amount of work involved in wiping out Mau Mau and capturing Haraka. He is also frequently embarrassed

---

[7] Eustace Palmer, *The Growth of the African Novel* (London: Heinemann, 1979), p. 313.

by the antagonistic attitude of people like Forester Jackson. Kingsley's impatience with his superiors is understandable. He is realistically portrayed as a thorough and hardworking officer, whose occasional outbursts only serve to underline his humanity.

> The captain stormed out of the uncomfortably hot tent into the late afternoon heat. He stood staring into the thick jungle across the trench, hating it, hating Haraka for getting away and hating his troops for letting him down. He hated himself too for ever having taken charge of the giant operation that was now slowly drawing to a painful conclusion, a complete flop. The whole damned thing a failure. (p. 128).

The passage reveals not only the captain's physical condition but also his state of mind. The captain is exasperated by the fact that, after such a "giant operation" it has not been possible to capture Haraka. So, he "stormed out of the uncomfortably hot tent into the late afternoon heat" — an action which does not improve his physical condition. When "he stood staring into the thick jungle...", hating everything and everybody, including himself, he is not helping mentally. The novelist intends that Captain Kingsley be seen as being physically fatigued and spiritually depressed at this stage. However, for the reader the situation described here is superbly ironical. At the time Kingsley is referring to his mission as "a complete flop", "a failure", Haraka is in great pains and at the point of death in his tent.

The novelist displays an exceptional creative energy in his treatment of the last days of Haraka. Both the language and sequence of events are extraordinarily attractive. Haraka is wounded by an enemy's stray bullet, retires to his camp to be nursed by his lieutenant, Kimamo, gets into a delirium and, in a feeling of mighty revenge, constantly asks for the head of his enemy, Chief Simba. Kimamo gets mortally injured in his attempt to carry out his master's orders and returns to the tent to die with his master. Nwangi records this tragic event in a moving and graceful prose-style.

> In the dark he was alone, cold and lost. And then suddenly he was not alone. Through the gloom he saw a tall, powerful phantom glide over to where he sat worn and lost. The ghost placed its hand on his weak shoulder and said comfortingly, voicelessly:

"Let's go."
"Where?" Kimamo's lips moved but no sound came.
"The gate", hoarsely.
Kimamo came to his weightless feet, and hand in hand the two floated joyfully towards the golden gates and the cool, dark jungles beyond. And the one who held his hand through the strange land led him into green places with merry, laughing streams and no angry bursting rivers and no pale-faced fierce soldiers, and no guns. The one who led him through the new place, as he had always done, was the general, his general, General Haraka.

We are thus provided with an imaginative description of Haraka's end. The general is lifted, as it were, from where he lies prostrate in the tent and brought before our eyes. There is a cinematic quality about the description which seems to preserve Haraka in the reader's imagination for all time. He is undoubtedly a memorable character.

IV.

The language used in *Time of the Butcherbird* reflects the gravity of the theme and constitutes an essential part of characterisation.[8] La Guma highlights the on-going dialogue of violence, in psychological and physical terms, between the blacks and whites in South Africa. The situation is so grave that one feels a major explosion cannot be postponed for much longer. The events of the book are ordered in a way to emphasize this inevitable catastrophe. The social gulf between the races remains as wide as ever. There is hardly an indication of compromise or accommodation. Pass laws, excessive taxation, high bus fares and unfair treatment of chiefs cause great irritation to the blacks. The Boers misconceive their role and abuse their power.

On one hand, we have Boers, who claim divine right for all the atrocities they perpetrate against the blacks in South Africa. On the other hand, there are blacks, who are inflexibly resolved to take their destiny in their own hands and kick against injustice.

---

[8] Alex La Guma, *Time of the Butcherbird* (London: Heinemann, 1979). All page references are to this edition.

The immediate cause of annoyance in this case is the government order to move Hlangeni's people from their land which has been declared an industrial zone. The novel is constructed around the people's resistance and the psychological and mental torture which accompany such a relocation. Kobe brings out clearly to the Bantu Commissioner the reality of the situation.

> We have been told that we must go from our land, from the land of our ancestors. But it is a very difficult thing to uproot an old oak of many years. The roots of such a tree are very deep. Certainly one can take an axe and cut down such a tree, that is easy, but the roots remain and are very hard to dig up. So you see, the tree really remains. The tree goes on.

Kobe uses language appropriate to age, setting and circumstance. His reasoning cannot be faulted. He uses the imagery of the oak tree to buttress his point and establish the claim of his race to the land "of our ancestors". The argument is clear and simple. A parallel is drawn between the blacks and "an old oak", whose roots "are very deep". The whites, may, through violence "cut, down such a tree", but "the tree goes on". The passage reveals, through the use of metaphors and analogies, the inflexible resolve of the blacks to remain at all costs on the land that is theirs by right and ward off the encroachment of the whites.

Given the differences of opinion and the social and political separation of the races, it is inevitable that racial bigots on both sides should exploit the situation for their narrow sectional advantage. It is not surprising therefore, that a feeling of uncertainty prevails. There are threats and counter-threats developed against a background of gloom. To achieve harmony between content and approach the novelist adopts, as appropriate, the language of satire or the attitude of despair or disapproval. Satire is appropriate to a situation, where people become so engrossed with thoughts of their own narrow interests, as to refuse to recognize that their world is crumbling around them. The whites will not face reality; at least, not openly. But there is Tant' Philipa, who secretly consults a black diviner. She is the object of La Guma's bitter satire because she will not treat blacks as equals, but fears them because of their ability to return evil for evil.

Other characters are satirized. Edgar Stopes is presented as a self-centred businessman. His only interest in people is the profit he makes out of them. He does not like the Boers, but he has to interact with them in the normal course of business. He lives in a world all his own and is generally oblivious of the social needs and convenience of other people. He hardly recognizes the signs of the approaching catastrophe; he is too busy with himself to come to terms fully with the world around him. His wife, Maisie, is self-seeking and morally bankrupt. Another important object of satire is Hannes Meulen, the prospective parliamentary candidate, who is responsible for the unjust imprisonment of Shilling Murile. With a diminishing sense of justice, he cannot be relied upon to represent the interest of all sections of the community adequately in parliament.

Mma-Tau is the symbol of black resistance. Because of the novelist's sympathy for the oppressed, she is built up into a monumental figure. She is "the she-lion, as ferocious as ever... a terrifying woman." (p. 46) She keeps up the momentum of the resistance at a time her brother, Hlangeni, is demoralised because he has recently been deprived of his chieftaincy title. He analysis of the situation in South Africa shows her deep psychological insight into the problem of her people, especially the heavy burden placed on them by the whites.

> They exist in a false happiness of guns and laws, they exist with false laughter, for the laughter is not really theirs. Do they know the meaning of their laws and their false happiness and their undignified laughter? The meaning is this: that men are of two kinds, the poor who toil and create the riches of the earth; and the rich who do not toil but devour it. The meaning is this: that the people demand their share of the fruits of the earth, and their rulers, of whom the white man is a lackey, a servant, refuse them a fair portion. And it is this: that the people insist, the rulers deprive them of work, drive them from their homes, and if they still resist, send their lackeys to shoot them down with guns. (p. 47).

Mma-Tau, in this slow but moving speech, analyses the situation in a way her largely illiterate audience can understand: there are two nations in one, the poor and the rich. The poor "toil and create the riches", the rich "do not toil but devour it". The two are diametrically opposed to each other, meet only on the battlefield and employ the dialogue of the gun. The speech is intentionally inflammatory but describes in a vivid manner, the great gulf which separates the blacks from the whites in South Africa.

Mma-Tau succeeds. She becomes the embodiment of collective justice and enjoys widespread support. She is able at the height of her popularity to halt government forces, an experience which stuns a police sergeant. "Who would have thought that these bloodly Kaffirs would start something like this? He had been defeated by a lot of baboons in jumble-sale clothing. What was everything coming to?" (p. 112). Even Shilling Murile and Madonele, who are at first cynical about her prospect of success, finally acknowledge, that she is making significant contribution to the liberation of the black people in South Africa.

La Guma uses the drought as a means of bringing white South Africans face to face with reality. The absence of rain is a symbolic way of letting the Boers realize that their heritage of which they seem so proud may not, after all, be a perfect one. The fact that they have agreed to pray collectively for rain and even declare a national work-free day for this purpose reveals the seriousness of the situation. It is also "in character" with a people, who believe they occupy their land "like the followers of Joshua". (p. 58) The reason for introducing the drought is clear to the perceptive reader. It is to mock the Boers and bring them out of their state of mental stupor and arrogance. The novelist uses the occasion to satirize the whites. For, even when they assemble for their special prayer, it is not in any mood of great expectations or deliverance. It is in an atmosphere of gloom. They show very little confidence or hope in their own activities.

> Inside the church there was an immense hush. Thick carpeting deadened the sound of feet as the worshippers dispersed into the pews. It was still run in the old style, women separated from their men, and the front pews paid for by the important families. An austere yet expensive church, all polished stinkwood, teak and imbuia, and tall windows; with oak and pine for the lesser folk. The organ, when the service opened, boomed and trumpeted like the hosts of Heaven, while the Dominee in gown of mourning black with double row of black tassels, ascended into the pulpit like a dark messenger come to announce the death of God. (p. 104).

La Guma's language brings out clearly his satiric intent. Segregation is introduced to the church in the way women are "separated from their men" and front pews are occupied only by "the important families". The organ which "boomed and trumpeted like the hosts of heaven" contrasts sharply with "the Dominee in gown of mourning". The priest is described as "a dark messenger come to announce the death of God". Certainly, this is not the kind of meeting from which any good can result.

Dominee Viser's speech on the superiority of one race over another cannot help the Boers. It is an exercise in futility and self-delusion. With increased resistance on the part of the blacks, and given the intransigence of the whites, one can hardly hope for a peaceful solution to the racial war in South Africa. In fact, it may well be, as the novelist is anxious for us to believe, that the time of the butcherbird is fast approaching.. Unfortunately, meanwhile, the suffering of the people continues unabated. La Guma evokes a picture of despair and gloom in his description of the circumstances in which his people have found themselves.

> This was no land for ploughing and sowing; it was not even good enough to be buried in. The people stood in the afternoon burn of the molten-metal sun, the scorching air turning the sweat and dust to plaster on their faces. They shuffled in the dust and gradually dispersed a little way from one another, looking about speculatively. An infant wailed thirstily in the sling on a mother's back, a child complained, someone spat out dust and hummed the opening bars of a song; another joined in and after a while everybody was singing. At least one could sing in this wretched and deserted lane.

V.

An attempt has been made in this paper to establish a link between language and theme in three African novels. Among them, these works highlight matters of cultural, social and political significance. The aim has been to show that whatever the theme or location in Africa, an appropriate use of language is essential for success.

A close examination of the themes reveals their variety. *The*

Slave, is based on a domestic theme of the forces within the clan which impede a man's progress. *Carcase for Hounds*, deals with the fortunes of a nation during a period of emergency. *Time of the Butcherbird*, has a more broadly based theme — the relationship between two racial groups in a state of conflict. This theme is international by implication, and the fact that it is an explosive one is implicit in the way the novelist handles his material. In respect of each of the novels treated, the author has for the most part adopted an approach and style suitable for his artistic purpose.

Confrontations and conflicts play an important role in these novels. They provide the occasions for the attractive passages of introspection, description and narrative continuity. These provisions assume great dimensions in, *Time of the Butcherbird*. This novel is, in a sense, a dramatisation of the limits of language. In his attempt to give a rounded picture of a people unwittingly moving towards tragedy, La Guma deploys his characters down a linguistic ladder from the loquacious Edgar Stopes to taciturn Shilling Murile. Again, language varieties in this novel, as in the other two, are accurate reflections of the status, setting and circumstance of the speaker. In all these cases, language is so thoughtfully employed that it becomes not only a means of effective communication, but also a vital link in the process of creation which gives meaning to a work of art.

www.ingramcontent.com/pod-product-compliance
Lightning Source LLC
Chambersburg PA
CBHW011139290426
44108CB00020B/2692